Cultural Intelligence in Practice

Expert insights for trainers in a
multicultural, globalised world

Lucy Butters

Cultural Intelligence in Practice

ISBN 978-1-917490-04-7

eISBN 978-1-917490-05-4

Published in 2025 by Right Book Press

Manufactured by
Sue Richardson Associates Ltd.
Studio 6,
9, Marsh Street
Bristol
BS1 4AA

info@therightbookcompany.com

EU Safety Representative
eucomply OÜ
Parnu mnt 139b-14
11317 Tallinn
Estonia

hello@eucompliancepartner.com
+33 756 90241

If you read one book on cultural intelligence, make it this one. Lucy Butters distills the wisdom of the world's cultural intelligence experts to offer a practical guide to securing lasting change across communities and continents.

— Baroness Wendy Alexander, vice-chair, British Council, UK

An excellent addition to the literature on cultural intelligence packed with practical tips for facilitators, teachers, coaches and anyone else who wants to help others learn more.

— Dr Linn Van Dyne, founder & CEO, Cultural Intelligence Center, USA

A future classic for anyone who wants to be an effective cultural intelligence or intercultural competence trainer. This book stands out for its wealth of real-world anecdotes drawn from the author's extensive work with diverse audiences across multiple countries. The depth and richness of these stories not only brilliantly illustrate key concepts but also offer practical insights that are immediately applicable in training spaces.

— Prof Michael Goh, endowed Campbell leadership chair in education and human development, and former vice president for equity and diversity at the University of Minnesota, USA

Far more than a theoretical text, Lucy Butters has curated a rich collection of lived wisdom and practical insights, with every page offering guidance grounded in real-world complexity and fuelled by hope. It is an invaluable companion for anyone who seeks to make the world better through human development.

— Chika Miyamori, chief culture officer, Ideal Leaders Inc., Japan

Told with a rare blend of wisdom, humility and global insight, this book is a gift. The reflections from real-world experiences make it not just a guide, but a true companion for anyone who trains or facilitates across cultures.

    – Quinton Pretorius, founder/director, CQ Africa, South Africa

A thoughtful and practical guide that meets you where you are, whether you're new to cultural intelligence or already have experience in the field. This book is not just something you read once and shelve; it's something you return to time and again. Lucy Butters has done an excellent job of translating complex ideas into an accessible, grounded resource for trainers and people practitioners alike.

    – Amanda Arrowsmith, people & transformation executive, UK

This book bridges the gap between understanding cultural differences and transforming how we work together. Lucy Butters has distilled wisdom from global experts into a framework that is both research based and immediately applicable, making it a practical, insight-rich guide for anyone committed to helping others thrive across cultures.

    – Des Ong, managing director, The Future Leader Group, Australia

For Viviane

Contents

Introduction

I n Greek philosophy, Aristotle used the term *'eudaimonia'* to mean human flourishing and believed the pursuit of improving yourself was the one virtue worth pursuing for its own sake. Cultural intelligence is about improving yourself in order to improve human interactions – the very definition of cultural intelligence (also known as CQ, the cultural intelligence quotient) being that we can relate and work effectively across cultural differences (Ang & Van Dyne 2009). This means any, and all, cultural differences. As soon as we get into groups, we start to create culture. Who speaks first? Who is heard? How are decisions made? Is there small talk? Humour? Snacking? Which behaviours become group habits? Which become the unwritten rules of how we do things around here? Which become our shared expectations?

Culture is everywhere, at every level, from broad categories such as nationality, religion, ethnicity, organisational, to smaller groups such as community, team, family and club. It is human beings in groups. As such, it is complex. Cultural intelligence is the capability to navigate that complexity.

As you have picked up this book, my assumption is that you may be someone who, like me, is involved with developing people and enabling others to flourish. I work to enhance international effectiveness and inclusive behaviours. I'm fortunate to have undergone a lot of training about working across cultures. I always enjoyed it and took away one or two useful nuggets. However, when I discovered CQ in 2013, it became my approach of choice as it gave me a framework to keep layering in my development and a real understanding of what was required to be a person who has the capabilities to bridge differences well.

I am now a master facilitator (currently one of ten in the world) with the Cultural Intelligence Center,[1] and was part of the inaugural group of CQ Fellows,[2] along with having my own business which develops people and organisations to be more effective working across cultures.

This is a book aimed at people who train (facilitate, teach or coach) and is written from that perspective. However, you may be involved in other roles that call you to develop others to work better across cultural difference, such as human resources (HR) or leadership roles. You may be as familiar with cultural intelligence[3] as the people who contributed their expertise and thinking to this book, or it may be new to you and you are curious as to how it could add to the work you do or indeed contribute to your own development. What I always find is that people who engage in developing the capacity of others to do well is that they are endlessly curious and always looking to develop themselves.

Whatever I am involved with, whether conversations in my family or working with organisations to support their people to be more inclusive and effective internationally, I've found that building my CQ has contributed to enabling me to engage and interact better with others.

Each time I facilitate a programme rooted in cultural intelligence, I learn from the discussions and insights that people share. Each time I'm fortunate to have discussions with other people who provide training with CQ, I learn from their approaches. I want to

---

1 I write in British English, but am using American English for this American organisation. I often hear people talk about right and wrong spelling, rather than different. Does the use of British or American English have an impact on you? If so, just observe it.

2 CQ Fellows is an elite CQ certification led by Dr David Livermore: davidlivermore.com/cq-fellows

3 There are more than 1,000 peer-reviewed papers on cultural intelligence conducted across more than 150 countries and published in more than 600 scholarly journals. Search for the writing of key academics in the field such as Dr Soon Ang, who pioneered and wrote the foundational works on CQ. (Nanyang Business School, NTU, Singapore URL: ntu.edu.sg/clci/our-people/soon-ang). There is also a selection of papers available at culturalq.com/about-cultural-intelligence/research

keep learning how to improve and one way of achieving that is to learn and share with others.

An idea took root that there were excellent trainers around the world with expertise in CQ, and if I could interview them, I would then be able to share their insights with you and explore how they use CQ in their work and their delivery of CQ training. Each conversation I had about this idea reinforced that I'm not alone in the desire to keep improving in this field.

Imagine you could draw from more than 100 years of experience and expertise to support you to build and use your cultural intelligence so that you can more effectively share it with others.

That is the intention of this book.

At its heart, this is a book for people who want to impact the development of others. The lens being looked through is the capabilities of cultural intelligence. It is about how we equip people in groups to flourish among themselves and with other groups of people.

My route to becoming a master facilitator in cultural intelligence

In 2013, David Lock asked me to design a training day he could offer to universities in the UK using cultural intelligence to support professionals in their international work. At the time, David was the director of international projects for the Leadership Foundation for Higher Education.[4] I had my own business as a trainer and coach supporting people working across cultures.

I had never heard of cultural intelligence. Not wanting to say no to the business and sensing that David and I were talking about the same outcome, I said yes. I am so glad I did and it didn't take long to discover that CQ was a specific approach to building our capacity to relate and work effectively across cultural differences.

My stars were aligned for, as fate would have it, Dr David Livermore was due to deliver a cultural intelligence certification

---

4 In 2018, this merged with the Higher Education Academy and the Equality Challenge Unit to become Advance HE in the UK.

programme in Edinburgh, not far from Glasgow, where I live. Once I had discovered CQ, it made me reflect so differently (and usefully) on my own capability to work well with others. It became the approach of choice for me: having thought I was highly capable at international work, the CQ certification programme made me look again, reconsider, and gave me a framework to improve myself.

I took all the CQ training that was available and went to the gatherings for facilitators. In 2021, I was invited to become a master facilitator with the Cultural Intelligence Center in Michigan, US, embarking on a programme where I developed my knowledge and abilities to deliver their certification programmes through working and co-facilitating with their master facilitators.

Prior to starting my own business in 2010, I worked for the British Council, which is the UK's international organisation for cultural relations and educational opportunities. I was always based in the office in Edinburgh, yet I credited my time with the British Council for turning my eyes out to the world.

I interviewed hundreds of international postgraduate students who had come to study in Scotland; mentored students and their host organisations during end-of-study work experience programmes; worked with colleagues in China, India and the US to develop and deliver marketing plans for the post-school education sector in Scotland; and worked with colleagues across nine Arab countries to deliver a leadership for community development programme.

Seeing the impact of that programme on participants and what they went on to do inspired me to establish my business in 2010, focusing on training and coaching, which initially focused on developing people to support internationalisation within universities.

While my roles with the British Council required that I work with people from anywhere in the world, I realise that my disposition to be open to people and the world started with my parents. My dad was a Church of Scotland minister in a small, rural town in the north-east of Scotland. I have a memory of answering the front door of our house, which was the manse in the centre of town. I was young, of primary school age. My memory is of being met by the smell of an unwashed man with lots of unkempt facial hair and layers of dirty clothing. I have no memory of what was said, but I do know that he left. My other memory linked to this event is how disappointed I felt that my dad was in me when he found out. My lesson was that no one was to be turned away from our door – and our home welcomed many guests, with many different habits and many different stories for us to observe and absorb.

I loved to hear my dad's stories, especially his tales of hitchhiking home to Scotland after working on a kibbutz in Israel, which he did on more than one occasion. He says that if you're wearing a kilt you can get a lift anywhere. (I've never tested this.) What always came through from my dad's stories was that he loved people and you could meet kindness, friendship and interest in people anywhere.

As a teenager in the 1980s, at a time when the Church was starting to lose the place it had enjoyed at the centre of many communities in the UK, I was aware that my dad was popular. When I questioned him about why this was so one day when we were out walking, he said that to get on with people you had to 'look out with love and respect'. I had no idea, aged 14, what he was talking about. With age I've realised how hard this is to live by, and 'looking out with love and respect' is one of the mantras I try to take into any space in which I'm training.

As an adult, I'm aware that I would have let my dad down, although he never expressed this. The only faith I have is in people (which, like all faiths, can be severely tested at times) and I have no belief in a god or desire to be within a religion. Walking and talking with my dad during a time when I was finding things hard, he said to me, 'Well, Lucy, you just have to be philosophical.' This has stayed with me. He talked to me in my language. He did not say he would pray for me, or tell me to trust in God – words that would have been important to him; he used language he knew would resonate.

Cultural intelligence is about being able to relate effectively with people who think about life differently than you do. I wonder if being involved in this field is not only about the professional aspects, but perhaps a personal quest to become more like my dad. Regardless, it's a quest that keeps opening up the world to me through the privilege of hearing people think through what developing their CQ could achieve for them, their interactions and relationships or organisation.

As I reflect on my route to, and interest in, CQ, I'm also aware that people come into my training holding many viewpoints and heritage stories. My starting point is my dad's mantra of looking out with love and respect.

Introducing the experts
who contributed to this book

Let me introduce you to the experts who were interviewed and contributed to the thinking within this book, briefly giving you a sense of where they are based and their main audiences and purpose. In the order people were interviewed (for no other reason than it was what suited schedules):

- **Dr David Livermore**: Based in the US, David is one of the co-founders of the Cultural Intelligence Center. He is a social scientist, speaker and author with a focus on leadership and cultural intelligence. In his role at the Center, he has delivered CQ training and keynotes around the world, with North America, China and South-East Asia being the areas he has worked in the most. While audiences and purpose have varied, key groups of participants have been middle managers, senior executives and people taking the CQ certification programmes. He is the director of the Society of CQ Fellows and consults with global organisations around the world.
- **Buhle Dlamini**: Buhle is based in Canada. He was introduced to CQ while working in youth- and faith-based work in his home country of South Africa, where he founded the company Young & Able. He now works globally (although his key focus is North America and South Africa), providing facilitation mainly

to corporate clients. He is also a sought-after keynote speaker on the themes of leadership, inspiration, culture and inclusion.

- **Dr Anindita Banerjee**: Anindita is based in India. Her key audience is multinationals, especially Indian ones. She mainly works out of India, but programme participants are from many countries. A key focus of her work with CQ is the synergies it has to support change management, particularly in the field of diversity, equity and inclusion (DEI) and/or enabling organisations to be more customer-centric.
- **Dr Fenny Ang**: Fenny is based in Singapore. She is a professional executive coach and consultant who has lived and worked in various countries, including Malaysia, China, Indonesia, the US and Australia. Her key client group has been multinational companies. Her focus has been on effective international leadership, and has more recently focused on female leaders who are managing transformational change in their teams, as well as successfully navigating cross-cultural terrains. She also has a focus on intergenerational leadership and collaboration in the workplace.
- **Andrej Juriga**: Andrej is based in the Czech Republic. After a career in sales and human resources at national and global levels for multinational companies, he founded and led Cultural Bridge in Slovakia, a training company that designs programmes predominantly for the corporate sector to help people become emotionally savvy and more efficient when working across cultures. He has lived in six countries across Europe and North Africa.
- **Justin Ngoga**: Justin is based in Rwanda. He leads Impact Route, which he founded in 2017. His company provides cultural orientation and CQ training to a diversity of clients, ranging from gap year and home stay programmes (frequently with participants from the US and Europe) to working with international companies that have operations in several countries. His driver is to upskill people and prevent the harm that cultural unpreparedness can cause in employee and organisational performance.

- **Dr Catherine Wu**: Catherine is based in Singapore. She is a lecturer in cultural intelligence and global leadership at Nanyang Technological University and the director of executive programmes at the Centre for Leadership and Cultural Intelligence in Singapore. She teaches the prestigious Nanyang Fellows MBA for senior public sector executives, as well as several other programmes. Originally from France, she started her career as a cross-cultural trainer in China. She is the co-host of the Cultural Quotient podcast, and producer of two others: CQ: Leading with Culture in Asia and CQ Weesdom.[5]

- **Samara Hakim**: Samara is based in the US. In 2014, she founded CulturGrit LLC to equip leaders with the mindset and skills, including CQ, to work with those who are different from them. Samara supports organisations to mitigate bias and integrate culture into their business practices and metrics. Samara grew up in Lebanon and draws on her personal journey, her legal career and her regular work across cultures to further organisational culture transformation and build more inclusive, innovative workspaces.

- **Tom Verghese**: Tom is based in Australia. He founded Cultural Synergies Pty Ltd in 1992. His key client group is multinational companies and there are three key elements to his consultancy: equity, diversity and inclusion; CQ; and global leadership. He has delivered development programmes in more than 40 countries, and his current focus is executive coaching.

- **Dr Sandra Upton**: Sandra is based in the US. Sandra spent 18 years working in universities, latterly as dean of a business school, prior to spending seven years as vice president (first for educational initiatives, then global diversity practice) with the Cultural Intelligence Center. In 2021, she returned full time as CEO to the business she founded, Upton Consulting Group, which uses CQ as a tool to design and create proven

---

5 The Cultural Quotient podcast: podchaser.com/podcasts/the-cultural-quotient-ideas-ti-5009686; CQ: Leading with Culture in Asia podcast: open.spotify.com/show/2eIdrkVR3fwqLTdkBXn1PL; CQ Weesdom podcast: open.spotify.com/show/3lY8sG5pN9PptgUdQopyEv

change management strategies that create inclusive cultures. She works with corporate clients across a range of sectors, from healthcare, retail, manufacturing and financial services to universities and governmental agencies across North America, Europe and South Africa.

* **Jennifer Izekor**: Jennifer is based in the UK. She is the CEO of Above Difference Ltd, which she founded in 2018. Their focus is on developing inclusive leadership and sustainable change, particularly within the UK's public sector, by designing development programmes that combine CQ, change management and values-based leadership to tackle internal and external barriers to inclusion and diversity.

Together they represent a group of experts with more than a century of CQ training experience between them. Appendix A lists their website details so you can explore each person's expertise.

I've gained so much by listening to these interviews and drawing insights from them. I hope the same will be true for you as you read on. When I first envisaged this book, I hoped to get at least six people lined up to interview. I invited 12 people; some I'd worked with, others I'd heard great things about during my years working with CQ. All received either an email or a LinkedIn message giving a brief synopsis of my intentions and a request to be interviewed. All of them said yes. Their willingness to share and contribute reinforced the impression I already had that these were people who wanted to equip others to enhance their CQ. Lyla Kohistany had to withdraw from contributing as an interviewee as she was dedicating her time to writing a thesis for her doctorate in education. Once she had completed it, she got back in touch to ask how she could support this project and contributed a chapter to this book (Chapter 11) instead – wow!

Moving into the scheduling phase was an immediate reminder to me that I had to use my CQ. I had not met everyone and my follow-up scheduling emails were in some cases not responded to at all. It dawned on me that my emphasis on getting tasks completed over building relationships was a specific cultural preference. A quick message to people from whom I hadn't heard, asking for a relaxed call so that we could get to know one another, changed everything. Spending time having a conversation about who we were resulted in people giving me a time for the interview.

While conducting the interviews, I was able to ask each person how they wanted me to address them. When I came to writing this book, I realised that if I wrote about some of them with their titles, and some by first name, that could be odd for you, the reader. I wanted the same approach used for everyone, so I'm using first names when the interviewees are mentioned in the text.

That immediately tells you something about my preferences around formalities and treating everyone the same. If it seems disrespectful to you that I only use a first name for someone I barely know who holds a PhD, observe that feeling. If you are wondering why on Earth I'm commenting on this, as you would use first names too, observe that feeling. In our choices and reactions to the choices of others, we often learn much about how cultures have shaped us. I like to tuck such observations away, knowing that the awareness will come in useful during an interaction at some point.

When I'm speaking collectively about insights drawn from the interviewees, the phrase I will use is 'the interviewees'; for example, 'All the interviewees agreed that building our CQ is a lifelong endeavour.' Again, some of the people who read early drafts felt this didn't confer the appropriate status on them. Notice what you think about this and what it tells you about how cultures have shaped you.

I am using the word 'trainer' throughout the book. Each of the interviewees was asked what word they preferred or used for what they did (facilitator, trainer, coach, consultant, professional development specialist were some of the terms given). Some had strong views about which word they used and why; others used the words (especially trainer and facilitator) interchangeably and were unconcerned by the descriptor. A couple of reasons for my choice to use the word trainer are that when I did my Certificate in Training Practice with the Chartered Institute for Professional

Development in the UK, there were several modules on the course and facilitation was just one element. Just as importantly, when reading advice on writing from the author Daniel Pink (2010), his suggestion was to read (or have someone read your words to you) out loud. Trainer is just easier to say than facilitator.

The Cultural Intelligence Center refers to me as a cultural intelligence master facilitator. However, when people ask me what I do, I typically respond by saying I'm a trainer and coach who supports inclusion and international effectiveness.

The interviews

After facilitating certification and train-the-trainer CQ programmes for the Cultural Intelligence Center, participants (who have since delivered their own sessions) sometimes contact me with questions.

- How do I answer a question like this…?
- What do you do when…?
- What needs to be considered if…?

These questions contributed to how I shaped the interviews.

The purpose of the interviews was to get a sense of how aspects such as audience, purpose and place impacted on how people worked with and shared cultural intelligence in their training contexts. I wanted to understand what might be similar or different in what motivated them, how they prepared, what they emphasised during training, what they found difficult (and how they responded to that) and what they had learned during their experience that they could share with you in this book.

Cultural intelligence is used as an approach for many different purposes, but they are all about human interactions and cultural difference. There can be many challenging questions from participants. Therefore questions were gleaned from a mix of open requests from me on LinkedIn, some in specific groups (there is a CQ-certified LI group) and from some interviews with people I knew were quite new to training in this field. Chapter 12 captures these questions and thoughts from the interviewees and me on aspects you may want to consider when responding.

I learned that conducting interviews is a skill in itself, and the interviewees came with very different approaches and styles – from concise, direct responses to expansive, intricate storytelling. Some asked before we started, 'How long do you want answers to be?' My response was always, 'Respond in the style that works for you and take the time you want.' And then I did not interrupt. Without exception, each interview was rich.

I so appreciate the time, generous sharing of experience and stories and the trust placed in me that I would draw the interviews together in a way that is beneficial. All of the interviewees share a drive to contribute to the flourishing of others. This book, however, is my responsibility. The words have been guided by the interviewees but I have chosen what to include, emphasise or omit.

How to approach this book

What I hope for you as the reader is that there will be an opportunity to reflect on your training practice or people development role and you can take suggestions and implement them to enhance your impact.

The four capabilities of cultural intelligence are:

- CQ Drive: your motivation and confidence in multicultural situations
- CQ Knowledge: your understanding of how culture can shape us and recognising cultural patterns and norms
- CQ Strategy: your planning for intercultural contexts and awareness of self and others
- CQ Action: your ability to adapt your behaviours and communication.

Whether these capabilities are new to you or not, this book gives you the information needed to understand how to build and use your cultural intelligence in your role and what the different elements of the CQ framework mean, along with tips, stories and suggestions for developing others.

Questions for you to reflect on are:

1. What am I **learning**?
2. What am I **thinking** differently about?
3. What **actions** can I take from this book?
4. How will this have **impact** for me as a trainer and the people with whom I work?

(Thanks to Rebecca Wilson, who uses these questions to review business books and kindly gave me permission to use them.)[6]

At the end of each chapter, I've included some key takeaways and questions to consider. You may wish to read all the way through the book or dip into specific chapters.

I'm aware that over the course of the three months that I was interviewing, I started to respond to some participants' questions differently. I found new ways of explaining aspects of CQ, which demonstrated to me that when we share and commit to learning with others we can keep improving.

What I'm also aware of is that I can't adapt the way I use my words to match this with your style. I don't know you or how culture may have shaped your preferences. A wise person shared with me that writing is not like training, where you can adapt to the people in front of you; writing is a one-way conversation. Therefore I'm asking that you use your CQ. When you find yourself thinking, 'Lucy isn't respectful, or humorous, or specific, or whatever enough', ask yourself, could that be to do with culture? What does it tell you about yourself, or suggest about Lucy's culture?

I'm a mum to triplet boys and have often found people asking me for parenting advice (as though having many at once conferred some specialist capabilities). I always say I'm happy to share stories from my experiences, but you know your context and situation. As it is with what is written here, the stories, tips and insights are offered as gifts for you to share, discard or restyle in ways that would work best for you.

6 Rebecca Wilson's Business Book Bites: youtube.com/@businessbookbites

Chapter 1

What's your motivation?

I want to help support people's change and transformation, and I think training is a great way to do that. – David Livermore

When I asked the interviewees what their motivation is for delivering training in cultural intelligence, I got to revel in their different tales of travel, of work challenges, of chance encounters and pursuits of knowledge and education. While each story is different, the common thread within each of the interviews is that cultural intelligence isn't the end point.

Cultural intelligence is the route, or an approach, to achieve a range of outcomes.

Change is always desired. As Anindita shared, even when an organisation reaches out specifically requesting training in CQ, she and her colleagues want to broaden that objective and develop the idea, to understand where it's coming from and to see it through the perspective of change.

Each of the interviewees had experience working in different parts of the world, with different sectors, with different people in different roles and stages of career or study, but there were two broad themes that were cited as the motivation for providing training in CQ, with some of our interviewees focusing on one specific purpose and others using CQ to support different purposes.

The two themes are:

1. enabling people to be more effective in their international ambitions (whether about relocation, international team productivity, study or global leadership)
2. enhancing inclusion (and that could be in a local, national or international context).

Equipping people to be more effective in their international ambitions

Working in various corporate roles in international sales and then HR, Andrej realised that he couldn't use his way of thinking to understand how others thought about communication, customer service or time. He lived and worked in five different European and North African countries and found each location had a different understanding of project management, a different understanding of strategic planning and a different understanding of people management. Yet he received no formal education or training to support him in understanding and adapting to different working norms from the companies he was with. Navigating the differences was left to his intuition, which sometimes worked but sometimes didn't. His company started to ask him to speak at their international events on how to make a success of relocating or leading an international team, and all the while he was thinking, 'Wait a minute – I have no theory or education informing my thoughts and practice.' This put him on a quest to find out what was out there that could inform his approach. It is a common story among the interviewees.

Catherine said, 'The motivation to get into the cultural intelligence space is more or less the story of my life.' Starting life in a small town in the south of France, where she says there was little diversity, Catherine had a drive to explore other countries from a young age. This was first realised when she studied English in England for a year. Interactions with friends made her question what influenced her motivation, and she began to recognise that our motivations are not just personal choices but the result of the society in which we live, such as the educational systems and expectations of family and the people around us. The impact of our cultural environments, which has been described as 'the collective programming of the mind' (Hofstede 1991) became evident to her in unexpected ways, such as how stressed or relaxed different friends were about exam results.

Setting her sights on a career in HR and supporting expatriates, Catherine travelled to China, where she had the immersive experience of adapting to a culture where it wasn't just that she couldn't understand the language, she also couldn't recognise any of the symbols of the written language. The struggle, stress and anxiety that came from having so few points of reference was very real to her.

Catherine designed and delivered her first cross-cultural training programme when the Chinese company she was employed by secured an opportunity to provide training to support a company working internationally. It was a two-day training event followed by focus groups. Catherine experienced a mix of being delighted to contribute and share what she knew, but also the frustration of hearing questions from participants saying, 'OK, you have shared models of culture and knowledge of how different nationalities are different, but how does this help me in my life where I work with teams made up of people from so many different places?' It was a question she recognised from her own life.

The tendency to reach out to people with experience is common. We see it in recruitment, who gets promoted or which trainers get invited to deliver sessions; there is often an expectation that the experience of being in a place, or working with a group of people, confers the skills someone will need. Without a doubt experience is important and we can learn much from the experience of others (it is the basis of this book)! However, what Andrej and Catherine both recognised was that they gained experience without gaining a clear understanding of what the essence was for enabling people to work effectively across cultural differences. Experience is far from being the only ingredient needed.

Professor Soon Ang worked with IT professionals during the 1990s. In the years leading up to the 2000 millennium, even people like me who had very little knowledge of computers knew there was a real concern that infrastructure relying on computing systems would be impacted negatively or brought to a halt due to issues related to the formatting and storage of data involving dates (the much-feared Y2K 'millennium bug'). Working with organisations who were recruiting IT programmers from around the world, Soon Ang observed that differences in working norms created conflict between the programmers and also between the international programmers' teams and local management.

While she had been working with organisations to enable them to recruit IT professionals who had both technical expertise and practical intelligence (defined by Sternberg et al in 2000 as four capabilities: managing self, task, career and others), what struck her was that the powerful yet invisible role of culture created another need.

The question that propelled her research into culture and intelligence was, 'How do people with vastly different norms and habits due to their cultural backgrounds work effectively with one another?' (Ang 2021; Chen & Steensma 2022) Her research led to our understanding of cultural intelligence today.

When Andrej and Catherine discovered CQ, they had that 'aha' moment of thinking, 'This is a framework that makes sense to me and gives me a tool I can share with others to empower them to navigate the complexities related to their international ambitions.'

For those of us whose experiences have led to us providing training and development for people navigating cultural complexities within international environments, whether business, personal or education, each of us had an experience that led us to the research about cultural intelligence. Once discovered, it became the approach of choice.

Enhancing inclusion

The question that led Jennifer to CQ was, 'How do we do inclusion better?' Inclusion was a driver for many of the interviewees, in different parts of the world. Cultural intelligence was viewed as an approach that enabled people to get under the surface of cultural difference to explore not just the difference, but crucially the capability to work effectively with difference in a way that leads to behaviour change.

Cultural intelligence is considered to be a powerful way to upskill people, to impact on changes in behaviour that could lead to sustainable inclusion. It is, of course, not the singular answer to creating organisations that are exemplars of inclusion, but it is a significant contributor.

I liked a metaphor Sandra shared of thinking of the change required to create organisations where diversity, equity and inclusion are in the DNA of the organisation as the umbrella. CQ is a crucial spoke. Without it, the umbrella will not work, but it requires other spokes to be functioning. An alternative way of looking at the umbrella may be to think of CQ as the shaft, which runs from handle to top, and which all the spokes are attached to. CQ contributes to the function of each of the spokes.

In their book *Getting to Diversity: What Works and What Doesn't* (2022), Frank Dobbin and Alexandra Kalev examine decades of data and research (mainly American data focusing on race and gender) into what companies have done that had a positive impact on getting more diversity into senior roles. They found the type of training that did have a positive impact was what they referred to as 'cultural inclusion training'. They described this as training that invited participants to think of themselves as being capable of developing skills to improve collaboration and communication within their settings, and being given tools to boost inclusion. While the term cultural intelligence is not used by them, the capability to collaborate and communicate well across cultural differences is the very essence of CQ.

Whether or not businesses are being effective across international borders can often be quantified with hard statistics around sales, recruitment or profits. Did the business achieve its aims? Diversity can also lend itself to easy, quantifiable metrics. However, inclusion can be a more abstract goal. It is not for me to tell you that you have been included; it is for you to tell me whether you have felt included – or even if you wish to be. Inclusion is about feelings.

I have had roles where I've been the only woman, or one of a very small number of women, and felt valued, productive and included. Conversely, I can also think of being in roles where I was in the majority as a woman but didn't feel any of us were taken seriously or would be considered for advancement.

Much has been written about what inclusion is, and my purpose with this book is not to define it. I like the phrase used by Dr Jonathan Ashong-Lamptey, CEO of UK-based company Element of Inclusion (elementofinclusion.com), who describes inclusion, in part, as ensuring 'everyone can perform'. What is relevant for this book is that CQ contributes to enabling people to plan and behave in ways that achieve inclusive workplaces.

Developing the CQ of leaders and teams upskills people to be able to think differently about how they plan interactions (around all areas of interaction in the workplace, be that feedback, recruitment, sharing ideas, engagement with clients and stakeholders, or chats with colleagues during breaks) and crucially the development to change behaviour, which can feed into everything from how we plan in policy development to how we listen.

What is also relevant to trainers, especially those working across borders, on the theme of inclusion is that, as Tom observed, while diversity is everywhere, inclusion is local. Mika Holborow is a trainer and coach with CQ certifications and a rich international life, having lived and worked in Grenada, Canada, Japan, the UK and, at the time of writing, Abu Dhabi, and she experiences how context shifts how you approach things.

The discussions and training using CQ in the UK that she had been part of had a focus on inclusive leadership. In Abu Dhabi, inclusion is considered through a different lens and has a different resonance in a land where the majority of workers are from different nationalities and there is no route to becoming Emirati; it's often more about respectful multicultural teamwork, leadership legitimacy and national workforce priorities rather than belonging in a Western sense.

It is important to think about the context you find yourself in. Language can change (sometimes rapidly), but the need for people to be able to thrive, contribute and perform, the essence of inclusion, is always present and necessary. Consider factors such as language, history, legalities and aspirations of inclusion in the contexts you will be training in.

Why cultural intelligence rather than other approaches?

Like myself, many of the interviewees had attended training as part of their careers working internationally and/or trained as trainers in different intercultural approaches. My experience was that I always enjoyed and took something away from any training related to intercultural working. However, it was not until I discovered CQ that I had a clear framework for developing myself.

That framework, with its four clearly defined capabilities, enabled me to make sense of the various snippets I had accumulated along the way. More importantly, the model was about my capabilities, rather than thinking of culture as being something out there. Think of 'doing business with…' or 'How to work with [insert demographic]' courses. These are useful, of course, but only focusing on building knowledge (or cultural awareness) is a limitation. This was a key point stressed by each interviewee.

Many were familiar with, and referenced, the work of social psychologist Geert Hofstede. When Catherine discovered Hofstede's work, she said it was like putting on a new pair of glasses. Suddenly, things that had been blurry came into focus. She had been aware that there was something different going on, particularly when she relocated to China from France and worked with international teams, but she had been unable to pinpoint exactly what those differences were. We can often observe the behaviours that are different to our expectations, but we don't understand what values sit behind the behaviours.

That focus on cultural difference is fascinating. It brings simplicity to something that can be abstract and vague. However, it still leaves the problem of how you use that knowledge. How will it help you in your everyday life? You've become culturally aware. So what? Now what? Cultural intelligence shifts the focus from only thinking about broad cultural groups to thinking about the individual capability to work effectively with cultural differences.

As one of the founders of the Cultural Intelligence Center, David has been involved in the research about CQ from the early days of research in this field (the CQ concept was first formally introduced in Earley & Ang 2003). What makes him interested in the research on CQ is the question 'How does this actually help people?' Taking the research out of academic journal articles and into training contexts has been a dynamic way of testing out the research and then using the questions and reflections that came back as a way of informing future research. Research informed by both science and practice has been central to the development of CQ since its inception (Ang 2021).

Only some of the interviewees had been involved in research relating to CQ, but all were aware of, and respectful of, the research. It is not necessary to have an academic understanding of the research to be an impactful trainer, but it's useful to know the key points about what the research has found in your area of expertise. Being able to link it to stories makes it stick.

When I attended the CQ certification programme in 2013, David shared that being involved with IT professionals in the 1990s during Y2K was the trigger for Professor Soon Ang to start her research. Linking it to other challenges that require collaboration across cultural differences (climate change, global supply chains, rapidly shifting demographics in societies) hooked me in. It only takes a few sentences, but it makes the research relatable.

One of my key client groups is the university sector in the UK, so the fact that there is an academic paper trail behind the CQ framework is important to me. When I'm working with academics, they typically want to know about the research or at least where to find it. My experience when working with businesses is that they want the practical application without the history of the research behind it.

Of course, CQ is not alone in having research sitting behind it. There has been robust, insightful and enriching research in many academic fields relating to culture and its impact. As a trainer in CQ, my view is that you do not need to be an academic or expert in all the research. Whether you can wax lyrical about etic or emic approaches (terms used in academic fields as to whether culture is being described from an internal or external 'scientific' perspective) is not necessary, and in most contexts would be offputting to your participants.

It is useful to observe and question whether people are applying universal principles from their understanding of a culture, whether they are seeking to understand a culture from the perspective of those within it, or whether they are applying learning from one culture and assuming to apply it everywhere. When I read articles on themes such as how to get ahead in business, for instance, it often seems that all the input for the data and thinking has come from one context, frequently the US, yet it is written about as though it's universal, without any testing.

Professor Soon Ang (2021) writes that CQ research comes from many academic disciplines: 'Scholars from more than 20 academic disciplines (including management, social sciences, economics and finance, arts and humanities, decision sciences, engineering and medicine) have cited CQ in journals, proceedings and book chapters... and spawned doctoral theses across the myriad disciplines.'

The research in CQ has also resulted in the ability to measure the CQ capabilities, which gives trainers the opportunity to offer participants individual assessments and feedback and also the potential to use assessments at different times to see if the training and development programmes are having an impact at an individual level. (I will return to this in the next chapter.)

The key point stressed by each interviewee is that the CQ research has resulted in an approach that enables people to develop their capabilities and move beyond awareness. Crucially, the research is not only about the concept of CQ or the development and validation of the CQ assessment, it is about outcomes. Research conducted around the world demonstrates the outcomes of developing CQ, including:

- trust, cooperation and negotiation effectiveness
- leadership effectiveness and work performance (individual and team)
- high-quality decision making
- adjustment and resistance to fatigue/burnout
- creativity and innovation
- profitability and/or cost savings.

Which of these researched outcomes resonates with your 'why'? Know the value of this. There are many ways to contribute. It's not about diminishing other approaches; it's about having clarity that CQ is about capabilities and is a proven approach.

Cultural intelligence enables trainers to invite people in and set the scene for them, to build skills, to change habits, to disrupt the pattern of unhelpful assumptions or communications, and to see themselves as having the potential to enhance collaboration and communication within their contexts when working with cultural diversity. My experience and the many instances I've witnessed and heard about show that people also realise something about their personal relationships with family and friends. Cultural intelligence truly is a life skill.

While everyone I interviewed was an advocate for CQ and used it in their training and development programmes, not everyone would always mention it explicitly. The reasons given for this were around purpose, ownership, context and familiarity with language.

Sometimes, if you are an external trainer invited in to work with an organisation, you do not have control over the name of the programme you are being asked to contribute to or the terminology that the organisation prefers. However, it may be that the purpose still resonates with you and you can still structure training around the four CQ capabilities of drive, knowledge, strategy and action to achieve that purpose; and as a trainer, you can demonstrate CQ in action.

Linking back to purpose being key, when I first started my training business, I ran public, one-day open training aimed at the university sector titled 'Enhancing Internationalisation'. It was a way of gaining traction and seeing if I could attract people to training sessions about the human skills we need to be effective internationally. When I discovered CQ, I was delighted with this newly acquired approach, which made so much sense to me. I titled my next open training day 'Cultural Intelligence' (omitting references to internationalisation), offering assessments for participants, and received zero registrations! It was a lesson in the importance of language. People in the UK had very little awareness of cultural intelligence in 2013, let alone what the purpose of it might be. While 'internationalisation' is an abstract term, it was a word universities were familiar with and had strategies about, even if different universities had their own way of thinking about it. Cultural intelligence had little or no resonance. I had not started with the 'why'.

Justin finds the same in Rwanda and so, while he uses the CQ model in his training, he often talks about cultural awareness as that is what people recognise and respond to. As an entrepreneur, he uses the language that resonates and attracts people to his training programmes. Culture is about context. Look out for and recognise the context you are in and respond with what will enable you to share CQ. Some of the interviewees found the opposite, particularly those working with leaders in different places around the world. 'Who wouldn't want to be on a programme where you can say you have increased intelligence?' as Tom put it.

I've been part of conversations where people are seeking to create a culturally intelligent organisation and have started by rolling out short CQ training sessions and then received the feedback that they have been too abstract. Establishing the purpose of why you would want to be a culturally intelligent organisation is important for bringing people on board and having clarity around what people are working towards. As Samara said, that could look different from different places in the organisation, with leaders being motivated by the vision for the organisation and middle managers wanting their teams to work better together. My preference is to be explicit, engaging people with the purpose and the benefits of using CQ as an approach to enable them to reach their aspirations.

The lives of the interviewees had taken them across country borders and continents or taken people across borders and continents towards them. Their work roles had involved leading diverse teams and the recognition that when people think about tasks, about relationships, about best and worst in a myriad of different ways, it can make or break the ability of diverse teams and organisations to achieve their aims.

There is a shared understanding that those different ways are commonly shaped by culture. (I will return to that word, culture.) Simon Sinek (2011) says that people engage when they buy into the 'why' of what we are doing. The 'how' (the CQ approach) and the 'what' (the training or development programme) comes after defining the 'why'.

Key takeaways

✧ Developing CQ is about contributing to change.

✧ The research is clear: developing CQ contributes to outcomes that demonstrate people are able to relate and work more effectively across cultures, both within and across national groups.

✧ Build awareness of your route to CQ and why you want to share it so that you can connect with others.

Questions to consider

✧ What is your motivation for delivering training designed to enhance the CQ of others?

✧ How would you express your purpose in a short (less than a minute) pitch?

✧ What research do/can you use to support the purpose of your work?

Chapter 2

Steps to take before designing CQ training

OMV: objectives, measures, values – that's always my opening.
That's always the thing I enter any client relationship with.
– Tom Verghese

The more time you take to really understand the impact a client wants to achieve (be that in the organisation you work in or as an external delivery partner), the more chance you give yourself to develop people well. This chapter is all about how this exploration stage may impact aspects of design.

The key questions that were asked of the interviewees were:

1. What questions do you ask your client?
2. What questions do you ask of yourself before delivering any training?
3. Do you use CQ assessments?

The interviewees were selected due to their expertise in CQ training. You may be reading from a different perspective. The first two questions are always useful, and the third is aimed at those wanting to develop other people's CQ.

What questions do you ask your client?

Four key elements came from the responses to this question: the challenge, the context, the people and the measurement of impact.

When invited to provide training, all of the interviewees wanted to explore what the challenge was that had prompted a request for training. Most of them are approached for reasons such as developing global leaders or effective teams, or to enhance diversity, equity and inclusion in organisations. It wasn't the norm for the terms cultural intelligence or CQ to be in the language of the organisation making the request. However, even the interviewees who were known specifically for their expertise in cultural intelligence would choose to further explore a request, which was often presented as 'We want you to deliver cultural intelligence training'.

Understanding the challenges and/or opportunities that the individual or organisation was seeking to address was key for all interviewees. What is the change you are contributing to?

What was going on that created the request for training? Had there been negative publicity? A restructuring of teams? A merger? Disappointing staff or customer feedback? Is there a new ambition or strategic direction to enter new markets? Does the organisation want to be more customer-centric, an exemplar of inclusion, or expand their talent or leadership development portfolio? It's crucial to build knowledge of the context the organisation and its people are operating in.

The interviewees shared experiences when they had been approached to provide training for one thing, then in exploring the context realised that there were many factors that would impact how successful training could be. An interesting aspect of interviewing people in different parts of the world, operating for different purposes and with different audiences, was that stories were shared that were different in detail but very similar in essence.

Justin, who was working with international African businesses to enhance intercultural skills, would come across similar scenarios to Sandra, who was working with US-based companies to enhance diversity, equity and inclusion. Organisations wanted to address a challenge with training, but in exploring the context, they were finding that the lack of trust, progress or poor communication between different teams or groups within the organisation needed much wider consideration than the skills development of a few people. It required organisations to be thinking more widely about processes and practices related to recruitment, promotion and access to training and development, for example. As Justin said, challenges relating to power and ownership are not going to change if there is only a short training intervention.

Understanding the challenge and context enables you to be clear about what you can have an impact on, how long you would need to engage with people, over what time period, who may need to engage with development and crucially to manage expectations – both yours and theirs.

Another context linked to power and ownership that came up for some of the interviewees was that they had been approached to help improve relationships in companies that had been taken over and their new HQ was in a different country. Conversations revealed that a group was effectively asking, 'How can we control our new bosses over there?' or 'How can we make these people do it our way?' Both of these have a different nuance from simply improving working relationships.

Taking the time to explore what is going on within an organisation enables you to either reframe purpose and expectations of any training, or to go in prepared to raise what may be considered the 'sacred cows' or the 'elephant in the room' and facilitate a conversation around it. These metaphors were both shared by interviewees from various countries, meaning they were using questions to understand what typically couldn't be touched or spoken about (such as questioning leadership style) or an issue everyone could see or feel but was not explicitly addressed (such as a history of actions not matching communications).

It also gives an indication of how participants may feel about doing the training. Are people viewing it as a growth opportunity? Or are they on the defensive as they sense that they are being treated as a problem that needs to be fixed? Whether or not people arrive feeling enthusiastic or defensive about any training is important for you to know before designing how you will start and build rapport. Linked to how people may be feeling about the training is how they have been selected to be there. Those of us who facilitate CQ certifications for the Cultural Intelligence Center can see the difference in the room (be it virtual or in person) when it is a programme people have self-selected to join versus one where people have been told to be there (sometimes grudgingly). This potentially has as much impact outside the training room, with people feeling they have been denied an opportunity.

How many locations, or departments, will people be joining from or will you as the trainer be travelling to? What are the different challenges and contexts in each of these locations? There can be a tendency to develop programmes to roll out across organisations and locations, but while the purpose and general approach can be replicated, often the starting point, examples and discussions, language and priorities need to be modified.

What are the hierarchies between those joining the training? Responding to different hierarchies in the room was a theme that arose so often during the interviews that there will be a later section about it. In the meantime, as part of your planning and due diligence, make a point of understanding roles and hierarchies between the people joining training. Tom says he learned the lesson of political nuance early in his work, so some of his key questions are always about the organisational politics. What's happening? Who's involved? What's the power dynamic like?

It's important to find out about the people who will be attending any training you deliver. However, it is also important to remember that a benefit of not knowing the people in the room is that you don't go in with preconceived ideas or expectations.

I remember contributing a couple of days' training to a week-long development programme, and in the handover before

I started, I was given a detailed briefing of participant behaviours, particularly someone the previous trainer had found difficult and domineering. When the person interrupted to ask about something (I had said I was happy with being interrupted at the beginning), I recall that I was only half listening as I was thinking of strategies to ensure they didn't dominate. Then I relaxed, focused and engaged, and my experience with the participant and the group was great.

I have also had the experience of only learning after the training (on a day that didn't go so well) that the participants had refused to be in the same room together for the past year. That piece of information would have been crucial in how I designed the day, but it had not been shared in advance, which was a lesson to me to ask better questions. Spend time understanding the context and the dynamics between participants in advance and factor them into your design and planning, but also hold all your assumptions about people in the room with an open mind.

What are the values of the organisation? How do they manifest themselves in everyday behaviours? Are those values understood in the same way across an organisation or is there variation across groups and locations? What impact does that have? Intentionally taking time to understand an organisation's values enables you to tailor discussions, insights and learnings that are the most relevant to the organisation.

Are you raising awareness or developing skills?

A key question Andrej wanted an answer to was, do you want to build awareness about this topic or do you want to build the skill among your employees and team members? Most of the interviewees spoke about experiences where organisations wanted to see behaviour change, but what they had decided was that there was only time for a series of repeated one-hour webinars or a half-day workshop. It takes time to build skills and change behaviour. This was a point stressed by most of the interviewees, whether they were in a classroom setting or with organisations.

Many trainers love short engagements that raise awareness

about the potential of CQ to impact positively on leadership, international effectiveness and inclusion, and my experience over a decade is that it can be the starting point for building relationships with organisations and progressing to more impactful work.

However, it builds your credibility to be clear about whether an engagement is about skills development and behaviour change or about awareness. When I first started my own business in 2010, I felt I had to 'give organisations what they were asking for', even when I knew the outcomes they wanted weren't possible within the time they were giving me. It took time and experience for me to build my confidence and be honest about this. The interviewees had different experiences of this. Jennifer was clear from the start of her business: 'I want to know that the organisation I'm working with, or my client, is committed to a journey of moving towards becoming a culturally intelligent and inclusive organisation.'

It didn't matter which continent the interviewees were speaking from. They all sought to understand what the organisation wanted, and if it was behaviour change, they would recommend a programme of engagements that would enable reflection, building skills and confidence between them (whether through facilitating various training events, setting experiential tasks, discussions and/or coaching).

I am now clear in my conversations with clients about what different events can achieve. I don't always convince organisations, but I sense it's not just my credibility but also that of cultural intelligence as an approach that is on the line if I sell the idea that a few short hours will result in lasting behaviour change. The real work for organisations starts after any training or development work.

I want to stress that individuals can decide to make a change (or changes) in behaviour after a short training session; however, culture change in groups requires more investment of time, repetition and reflection to build that muscle of applying CQ, particularly when teams are complex, stressed or under time pressure. I want to share two illustrations of behaviour change after short training sessions.

One of the first programmes I worked on at the British Council was to select international postgraduate students and develop a business networking and placement programme for them. At the time, students from China were both the largest nationality group of international postgraduate students in Scotland and those in most demand from companies.

Each year, I would explain all about the visa we were going to be applying for to facilitate the work placement at the end of their studies and ask, 'Are you happy to go ahead with that?' Each year, after saying 'yes', one or two Chinese participants would then start another visa application. Having two separate applications for the same person was a disaster. They would both be thrown out and there was no way back from that. It used to confuse and frustrate me. To my thinking, people had been given all the information and agreed the way forward.

Then I attended a short presentation about 'doing business in China' where I learned that saying 'no' directly was considered rude. (There are, of course, lots of ways of saying 'no' in China; I just lacked the knowledge to recognise them at the time.) When I changed my question from 'Are you happy to go ahead with that?' to something along the lines of 'What do you want to happen now?', it created space for the conversation to explore different options and concerns. I never had the problem of a student submitting a separate visa application again.

Russell Dalgleish describes himself on LinkedIn as a 'Scottish serial entrepreneur' and among many things he is the founder and chair of Scottish Business Networks (SBN), which has created and sustains an ecosystem to support businesses based in Scotland access opportunities across the globe. I barely know Russell, having had one conversation when I met him at an SBN event in Edinburgh, yet one of his comments stayed with me. Thanks to LinkedIn, I was able to reach out and he generously gave me some time to check that my memory was accurate.

He attended a one-hour session about unconscious bias. It introduced a concept he had been unaware of. He realised that his love of listening to football commentary (you may know it as soccer) was lessened if the commentator was female, even if that woman had a wealth of expertise. Throughout most of his life, football commentators had been male and that had, unknowingly, created a bias. Russell made changes after that hour. He now refuses to sit on business panels if there are no women on the panel. Diversity of voices is an important factor in inviting people onto the many speaking panels hosted by SBN. It's simple and yet so often neglected (just take a look). Who we get to listen to shapes our sense of the world and who is worth listening to – gender being an obvious difference in all societies.

I have selected two examples that demonstrate how individuals can change a behaviour after a short session, and that change can contribute to a positive ripple effect on others. I've also chosen two examples that CQ trainers would describe as sitting within the CQ Knowledge capability (see Chapter 6 for more about this). However, knowledge in and of itself does not change behaviour.

People may have never heard of CQ but that doesn't mean they are lacking in it. It's important to never underestimate your participants. My preference when training is to create a framework where I'm frequently asking people about what they could do differently and to assume that people are going to take something away that they can meaningfully apply to their own context.

I take the position that individuals can change their behaviour (or add a new behaviour) after a short training session. When I changed my attitude from 'How would I present this?' (which used to be in my headspace when I attended training/presentations) to 'What am I going to take away and use?', it really shifted how I respond to any event. In most audiences, I'm aware that there will be a spectrum from people resisting everything you say to those who are actively looking to take away something practical.

However, the behavioural change required to create and sustain culture change across an organisation requires much more investment of time as it requires collective action. Linked to this is another common element from the interviews – the questions around how the training is being sponsored and supported within the organisation.

If you are providing a one-off team-building or awareness-raising event, then questions you could ask clients include:

* What prompted the decision to host the event?
* Who will be in the room?
* What is going on for participants in the organisation at this time?
* What has worked well in the past?
* What do you want participants to be feeling, saying or doing after the event?

If you are building a relationship with a client to develop a vision of what better leadership, or a more customer-centric or more inclusive organisation looks like, then the interviewees also suggested the following questions:

* Who has accountability within the organisation?
* Who do they report to?
* What is the budget? (Not for the training or your engagement, but for implementing the organisational goal. Note that this would not be responded to in all contexts.)
* How will the training and development be supported in an ongoing way?
* How will the organisation measure impact and recognise if the training has been successful?

If you have been reading this section about questions to ask clients, thinking it doesn't apply to me as I'm working in-house to deliver training, it can be tempting to skip the part of taking a step back and really exploring the challenge and opportunities, the context your organisation is in and how people may feel about it, but it is typically just as important and worth revisiting. Taking this time can also boost your part in influencing outcomes for your organisation.

What questions do you ask yourself?

When you have been invited to provide training, it's an opportunity to embody your own CQ. The interviewees spoke about how they drew on their CQ to consider their drive, knowledge and strategy, before moving to design.

CQ Drive was mentioned the most (see Chapter 5 for more about this capability). Are you curious about the opportunity? What is your motivation? Does it align with your values and purpose? Will the opportunity enable you to grow, to learn, to build your reputation? In other words, what is in it for you or your organisation, as well as the group receiving the training?

Many of the interviewees spoke of turning down potential work when it didn't align with their drive and purpose, and also about the importance of declining requests while maintaining positive impressions and relationships. The conversations you have with potential clients about what is driving them to provide training goes hand in hand with you developing your drive to work with them.

Along with understanding what draws you to training and the benefits you may derive from it, the third factor linked with drive is confidence. How do you rate your confidence (or self-efficacy) to deliver the training? Confidence isn't static and can rise and fall, with the interviewees sharing that their confidence may have been dented due to a bad experience while training a certain group or because they were overthinking aspects such as the seniority of the people. While working with universities, I often had moments of mini-crisis as I thought, 'I'm the only person without a PhD in the room!' I found that taking a deep breath and remembering I was invited in because I had expertise to share was the best way for me to deal with that. Likewise a (real or perceived) lack of knowledge about, or experience of, the sector, region or country they are being invited to could impact confidence.

As Buhle shared, first and foremost, everyone is human. Recognising that you have anxieties enables you to focus on building strategies to connect with your participants as humans. And as Samara commented, you do not need technical expertise in the field of the people you are training, as you have expertise in CQ and skills in training and that is what you are being asked to contribute.

The purpose, place or duration of the training impacted on what types of knowledge people sought in preparing themselves. 'I am data driven,' was a comment by one interviewee. For some it was strategy, mission or equality, diversity and inclusion policies; for others it was seeking what could be found in feedback online about the company and its leadership. When I was invited to Pakistan to deliver CQ training to different organisations, I spoke to people who had lived and worked there, who had delivered training and who could teach me some key phrases in Urdu. Finding a trusted person with experience of the place or sector was a strategy shared by many of the interviewees for building knowledge before entering into any training delivery.

Building our knowledge also contributes to our awareness (a critical factor for CQ Strategy – see Chapter 7), depending on the questions you ask about that knowledge. What assumptions do you have about the group and what assumptions may they have about you? It didn't matter what race, nationality or gender the interviewees had. What I heard during the interviews is that they take time to think about how they may be perceived due to aspects of their identity, particularly if they, as the trainer, were likely to be the only person with a particular identity trait. If you have enough of a trusted relationship with the client, you may even want to ask them, 'How are people going to perceive someone like me coming in?'

Fenny is a coaching supervisor, and a key skill from that experience is to learn how to do an almost third-party observation of yourself. Ask questions such as, are there parts of your identity that your attachment to impacts on your interpretations of words or interactions in this context? Is there anything in the brief that is making you feel defensive, joyful or uncomfortable – and where does that stem from? As Fenny said, it is incredibly difficult to observe and stop your own bias. You need to play the expert, while at the same time being a continual learner. To me, this would also sum up the essence of developing your CQ.

The benefits of working through these aspects of your drive, knowledge and strategy is that it enables you to frame introductions, session outlines, stories, examples and exercises used during the training in ways that minimise or amplify what is most useful. It also gives insights as to where there may be tensions, which means you can plan for them.

CQ assessments and measuring impact

Before her involvement with cultural intelligence, Dr Linn Van Dyne was head of the HR department at a multinational organisation. As part of her job, she sent many expatriates all over the world. They all had strong track records and were willing to go abroad, but in Linn's words, 'They were terrible at predicting who would be successful and who would fail. That was a problem.'

Years later, after she got her PhD, she worked with an international team in Singapore and developed and validated the Cultural Intelligence Scale (CQS), which assesses a person's CQ. The subsequent research has proven that this scale can predict cultural effectiveness. Dr Van Dyne is one of the founders and current CEO of the Cultural Intelligence Center. She is not the only contributor to this book who said that they wished the scale had been available when they were in a previous employment. (My thanks go to Linn for taking the time to talk with me and write to me about creating and validating the Cultural Intelligence Scale.)

Individuals can be invited to take a CQ assessment before attending training. On completion of the assessment, they receive a personalised feedback report, which they can either download themselves or you could choose other options so that you can plan for them to see their feedback at a specific point during the training. This CQ feedback report displays a person's capabilities across the four distinct areas of CQ as well as the 13 sub-dimensions, presented to show how you compare with others who have taken the assessment (at the point of writing, this is more than 250,000 people). Along with this evaluative aspect, there is a descriptive aspect about mapping preferences for ten cultural values.

When designing your training, you can select self-assessment or assessments where there is observer feedback for individuals. What many trainers also find useful is how these can be pulled together into anonymised group reports, which are great when working with teams.

The interviewees were mixed as to whether they used CQ assessments as part of their training. (You can purchase self-assessment CQ assessments at culturalq.com, and if you are a certified CQ facilitator, you can purchase 360° assessments that include feedback from observers.) Some always use CQ assessments, particularly those working with leaders or providing training for the Cultural Intelligence Center, which recommends that improving CQ starts with taking an assessment. Some worked with a number of different tools, which, depending on the purpose of a training programme, can be used alongside CQ. Some rarely or never used the assessments, while using the CQ framework as the approach.

Budget was quoted as the most common reason for not using a CQ assessment. Depending on where you are in the world or the types of organisations you work with, the extra cost may put the assessment out of reach. The budget available for the work you are doing may be too limited, particularly if the organisations are new to CQ and you are still proving your worth to them.

A couple of the interviewees said that they liked to use the assessments, but sometimes would have clients who did not want to use a tool with the word assessment attached to it or took the position that we 'should not be measuring people'. We need to work with the organisations we are in, or who invite us in, and how they respond to the potential of assessments is part of the discovery as to what will work best.

The assessment is not about 'measuring' people – it is about self-reported capability at a point in time when people take the assessment. As it's a developmental approach, it's about finding a baseline so that people can reflect on their own capabilities and make decisions about whether and how they want to develop. I've sometimes talked organisations out of using CQ assessments when they initially requested them – for example, in an organisation where teams had gone through various mergers and there was uncertainty and a breakdown in trust. The director wanted to use the assessments in the expectation that it would show everyone how much they had to develop. He had been introduced to the CQ assessment at another one of my training events and loved it. In terms of building trust, my sense (based on previous experiences of using the CQ assessments with a team where there wasn't trust) was that using any type of assessment wasn't useful in the first instance. Instead, we had a team-building day where the themes of trust and communication were explored using the CQ framework as the shape for the day. That led on to various other engagements with that organisation, where CQ assessments were used.

One interviewee stressed that cultural intelligence is complex, which means the feedback from an assessment is complex – therefore it was important to consider if the time you had available would enable people to understand their feedback and if there was a robust ecosystem around the training or to consider how many times you would be engaging with participants in an ongoing way, as part of the thinking as to whether or not they used them.

Linked to this is the need as trainers to ensure that participants feel safe within any training environment. A key part of this is ensuring that individuals never need to share their individual feedback. I always stress this. Have strategies on hand about how you'll respond to requests in the room to know who had what feedback. (There is often one person in the room who wants to know.) The anonymised group reports are especially useful with intact teams as this data can be shared without calling anyone out.

Another reason organisations may not want to use CQ assessments is that if they use other assessment tools, they don't want to introduce another one, even if they want to have CQ training and development work. This is true of some UK business schools I've engaged with. However, the CQ assessments are a great tool, with academic validity, which can add much to any training programme. I have found that participants frequently respond well to having their own individual feedback, or team feedback, to focus their reflection and planning on. However, like anything else, it depends on context.

- What is the purpose of the training?
- What are the issues facing the participants?
- What other tools are being used?
- What is the budget?

These are a few of the questions to have to mind when you are making the decision whether or not to use CQ assessments. If you are using them, it creates the potential to reassess at a later date as a measure of how the training is going. Some interviewees had used pre- and post-CQ assessments as part of the evaluation, typically stating six months as the minimum time period between first and second assessment.

When working with individuals on relocation coaching or leadership development coaching, using the assessment at different points can be worthwhile as an aid for reflection and noticing how the person is adapting and growing. It is also a great tool for universities, measuring the impact of programmes that were designed with the intention of building the CQ of students as a graduate attribute. If there are no changes in CQ, are the programmes working? What could be altered to build in opportunities for students to develop their CQ?

While the CQ assessments offer an opportunity to measure whether the training and changes organisations are putting in place are having an impact on the CQ of individuals, it is worth remembering that in the last chapter, the interviewees saw building CQ as an approach to facilitating change.

What is the desired impact of developing CQ? What measures will demonstrate that the impact is being realised? This could be linked to various data the organisation collects such as customer feedback, staff surveys, recruitment and promotion data, marketing and sales data. If you are an external trainer, you may not get access to this data, but you want to encourage the organisation to measure impact.

The credibility of CQ training generally, and for you specifically, is enhanced when it is clear that it leads to results. You cannot know that there are results unless organisations are measuring impact. You are fortunate to be working in a field where there has been much academic research and cited papers that demonstrate results, ranging from decreasing anxiety in culturally diverse situations to CQ being a key predictive element for effective leadership in diverse situations (Livermore 2024).

Key takeaways

✧ The more clarity you have about the purpose, challenges, opportunities, values and people attending training, the better you can tailor your design.

✧ Take time to acknowledge and understand your drive, knowledge and assumptions about any group you are working with. This can enhance your training delivery, enabling you to think through strategies on how you will build rapport, trust and credibility with the group.

✧ Be clear about what training can, and cannot, achieve.

✧ The questions you ask of clients enable you to design and tailor aspects such as structure, whether to use CQ assessments (and/ or other tools), practical/concept balance, examples and stories to link with purpose, activities that will resonate and how you will pace and revisit different elements.

✧ Clarify what will happen after any training around support, embedding and measuring impact.

Questions to consider

✧ What questions will you ask your organisation/client/colleagues to enable you to design the most impactful training for the context you are in?

✧ How do you use your CQ before designing and delivering training?

✧ When would using CQ assessments enhance the impact of your training? How comfortable are you with using the CQ assessments?

✧ What assumptions about yourself and the people you will be training serve you well? What assumptions surprise you or could you usefully explore?

Chapter 3

Finding a hook to engage your participants

As John C Maxwell wrote, 'Everybody communicates, few connect.' Make it your aim to be someone who's great at connecting with people. – Jennifer Izekor

This chapter is about the hook you use to connect with your participants. Each interviewee was asked, 'How do you engage people right from the start of your training?' As you'd expect, everyone said that could vary depending on purpose, audience and time. Most mentioned using storytelling and/or quickly getting participants talking or feeling something, but the themes of the stories or what they got people talking about varied.

Three themes emerged: purpose, human connection and concepts such as culture or leadership. There is another factor that wasn't raised explicitly during responses to this question but did come through in the interviews, and that was about establishing credibility. I have worked with trainers and organisations where this is the starting point, and as with the themes, how you go about establishing credibility with different audiences varies.

I'm sure that everyone would agree that purpose, human connection, key concepts and establishing credibility are all important and I'm assuming that everyone would include these aspects early in any training, but not every interviewee mentioned all of them, and what they chose to have interaction or tell stories about was different. How they went about engaging people from the off revealed what was emphasised and how they may go about bringing participants into the conversation.

I have found this to be a useful reflection. All three of the interviewees based in the US started with purpose, reminding participants about challenges and the reason for their being in the training space. I rarely start with purpose. I'm not suggesting that starting with purpose is the dominant American way – three people is just anecdotal. I'm sharing my reflections on the responses.

I realised that when the session is about working internationally, my hook is typically the concept of culture, and then purpose is the transition into the content; whereas when the session is about inclusion, I typically start with sharing far more about myself and what makes inclusion important to me, then asking participants the same, before moving on to purpose, depending on numbers. If there are lots of people, I might pose a question such as, 'What is one word that expresses why inclusion is important for you?' and create a word cloud or similar.

The Cultural Intelligence Center's programmes typically start with purpose, and I usually change the order of the training regarding when introductions are made, what they are about and when purpose is clarified. Listening to the interviewees has highlighted this for me and encouraged me to think about how my preferences were shaped and when they may be most useful.

What follows are some of the suggestions as to how the interviewees go about engaging participants at the start of training sessions, ordered within the themes that emerged from the interviews.

What are your go-to ways of hooking and engaging your audience at the start? When, how and where do you mix this up?

Purpose

David said that in the first five minutes he wants to be mentioning pain points, values or the insider lingo that he has picked up during his contracting conversations. Tom said that he opens with stories, always short and always related to an issue, a problem or a challenge the participants are dealing with. Depending on your brief, you may be speaking to a broad purpose (such as inclusive leadership) or a specific challenge (such as specific team productivity or dynamics within the cohort you are with), and so that becomes the prism through which you can open the training. The key message to get across is that this training aligns with the purpose of the participants and is a valuable use of time.

Anindita shared that, for her, the focus is sometimes on specific cultural groups, for instance when working to support a merger or new market entry. Therefore, from the get-go, she invites participants to share what impresses them and what annoys them about this group they are working with. It focuses participants on the purpose and also draws out perspectives that Anindita then weaves into discussions throughout the session. (She emphasised the importance of not sharing judgements when gathering input, especially at the beginning.)

I know CQ trainers working in-house with organisations who start by mapping the life cycle of projects or a typical day for their participants, then drawing out where the group have cultural challenges. (I often hear people focus only on challenges and problems, so it can be useful to highlight opportunities too. This speaks to my experience of working with an appreciative inquiry approach, which emphasises positive idea creation over negative problem identification. I suspect the preference, or norm, is both contextual and cultural.)

A useful way of connecting with purpose is to ask the participants what their purpose is for taking the training, which can be especially helpful when it's a training event that draws people from different organisations.

Human connection

Buhle has a standard introduction that he shares different versions of depending on time, but the purpose is always to share who he is as a human, and for him that is the story of family. He is

South African, now based in Canada, married to a Canadian. They have four sons, with a 27-year age gap between them. The oldest is adopted and originally from Congo; their second son is also adopted. He is also Buhle's brother, whom he adopted when their parents passed away. He and his spouse have two younger sons. In the South Africa Buhle grew up in, his family would have been illegal under apartheid.

Buhle intentionally doesn't mention his work credentials in his introductions. Typically, a brief bio will already be with participants and Buhle's sense is that whether they have read it or not, the fact that people are in a room with him suggests there is an acceptance that he has expertise and he doesn't feel the need to prove that.

His story brings the issue of diversity to the fore and he intentionally places it outside of any work perspective. His experience is that when he then asks people to share a little about themselves, they often draw from different aspects of their lives. Buhle had been working with senior executives at a bank not long before our interview. The feedback from participants was that they learned things they never knew about colleagues they had worked with for years and at the end of the session the takeaway was that they should be connecting and sharing as humans more often, as it shifted what they brought to discussions and how they interacted, in a positive way. All of us have a story to tell.

What you will notice with Buhle is that he has a purpose around the impact he wants his story to have when he shares it at the beginning of a training. It is a useful barometer for each of us as trainers when we share: what impact does it have on our participants? If it silences rather than opens up, then it is perhaps time to reconsider what we share or how we share it, to ensure that we do engage and bring people into a training space they can share and learn in.

A perspective on this approach is that we connect as humans and if we can be vulnerable and share as trainers, we encourage others to be open and share more, in order to understand more of each other and work better together.

Concepts and ideas

If the purpose is to enhance inclusion or international effectiveness and the approach is CQ, that brings concepts such as culture, CQ and inclusion centre stage. For those who hooked the audience with concepts first, it was often done with a question: 'How would you explain or describe the word culture?'

My experience of asking for one word from participants is that a long list of words is created (even when I let people know it's not an exercise in being individual and it's fine to repeat words that have already been used). Values, language, behaviours, belonging, uniqueness, food, religion, society, beliefs, traditions, history are just some of the words that are often shared. Take a moment to absorb those words. Are there any that you would say are not about culture?

Culture is such a small word and we often use it casually ('the culture around here is...'), yet there is so much complexity packed into it. We could easily spend a long time debating what we mean by words such as values, or whether all behaviours or beliefs are about culture, or pose questions such as, 'When much from history is forgotten, what elements determine culture?' Culture truly is complex.

Opening a session in this way enables you to get your participants' voices in the room, quickly open up the concept of culture and its complexity, and state that CQ enables us to navigate that complexity for whatever the purpose of the session is.

There are many variables on the above that you can mix up depending on audience, time and purpose. A word to describe the culture of the organisation could be followed by questions such as, 'Would all teams or departments recognise the same culture within the organisation?', 'What does inclusion mean to you?' or 'What is your "why" for being inclusive?'

Which request for a word, or words, would highlight a key concept of your training with CQ and get everyone to share their voice, even if information is shared anonymously with whatever technology you are using?

Andrej sometimes opens sessions by asking people to put their hands up if they are culturally intelligent, and then asking, 'Why do you not have your hand up?' Or, 'Why do you have your hand up?' It's a way of getting straight into the conversation on the theme of CQ. If you're going to try this, be sure to know your skills and audience, as when I heard this, I confess I thought I might have been terrified as a participant, before realising that I'd be in safe hands with Andrej! The purpose of engaging with the concepts at the start was to enable people to quickly share some thoughts and set the scene as to what the participants have in mind when talking about some of the concepts being raised in the training.

Establishing credibility

You want participants to relax and engage, and part of that is about establishing credibility. When the interviewees mentioned establishing credibility, place and audience were always part of their thinking. Many interviewees had experience of training in different parts of the world and commented that how they would go about establishing credibility would vary with location.

There's no definitive way to go about establishing credibility. Consider how much detail to share about your experience and your relationship with the company you are working for; whether to limit your introduction to a quick sentence and then show your expertise; whether to be self-deprecating or absolutely not to be; whether to lead with the research that underpins your approach or your experience of using the approach; and which elements of humour or personality you share in ways that will engage your audience and enable them to learn with you. Research the context of your learners. Two things to bear in mind, however, are to avoid pretending you're something you're not or have experience you don't. A few of our interviewees said, as I frequently do, that while I have expertise in CQ, I typically don't have expertise in the trainees' work environment or sector. I find it useful to be explicit about this.

Another note of caution I would share is that I have been in sessions where, by way of introduction, trainers have gone through a long list of countries they have lived in or shared a list of negative experiences they have had, without it being clear why they are sharing that information. I've witnessed this having the impact of silencing the room, making people feel they lack the requisite life experience to become culturally intelligent or become defensive, neither of which are great starting points.

Consider the purpose of the information you are sharing. What have you learned from your experiences? How does it link to the theme? Does it give your participants hope? It's always useful to think through which elements of your experiences are useful to share, especially at the start of any session, and how you want that information to impact on and engage with the audience. Then pay attention. Is it having the impact you had hoped for? If not, would it be useful to mix things up a little and try different approaches?

Listening to the interviewees, it was clear that audience, purpose and time are important, but also that trainers make assumptions and come to different decisions with the same information. Phrases such as 'these are busy executives' were used by the interviewees to state the importance of establishing purpose first (ie to establish why it's a good use of participants' limited time) and to say why it's important to focus on each of us as humans first, as their very business often prevented that, and then creating space to think beyond the business imperative to what enables them to interact more effectively.

Likewise, some interviewees used phrases such as 'you have to relate to the audience', but then chose different aspects to focus on to create that connection (be it purpose, human connection or concept). What's also apparent is that each of the interviewees is great at what they do. They get engagement, they do hook in their participants and get them ready to engage with the content. This is not about better and best, right and wrong, as each approach works. It's about building your awareness about your approaches, what works for you, and thinking of different options and when they may be useful.

Hearing from participants early on was stressed by most of the interviewees. As Catherine said, CQ is fundamentally an interpersonal skill, therefore it cannot be developed via a lecture. The opening is an opportunity to set the tone and expectation that there will be engagement and exchange. Going beyond asking people to just share their name and give a thought on purpose, concepts or their humanness is a good way to do this, and can be accomplished whether virtual or in person, between you and each person within the group, or between small groups who share with each other rather than you (when numbers are high and/or time is tight).

Creating movement so that people can think differently or experience a sensation as a way of creating space for people to speak was also a favoured opening tactic for some of the interviewees.

Examples:

1. Create a space that represents a continuum from 'agree' to 'disagree' (with a central space for 'don't know' or 'don't want to answer'). People can agree a little or they can agree a lot. Then ask people to move to where they are in relation to a statement you make. One example I have used is, 'People can get on with anyone if they mean well and are polite.' Emphasise that you are not going to be giving a right or wrong place to stand and let people move. Then move about and ask people something like, 'What thoughts made you stand here?'

   I have moved lecture halls full of students into corridors for exercises like this – learning that it is wise to give out all the instructions before inviting people to move! – and my experience is that once everyone is on their feet, it becomes a non-confrontational space and people do share their thoughts and experiences. People don't need to speak if they don't want to, but generally people do when invited, or offer to speak, or start to move as they react to different perspectives, which is a great observation for everyone.

2. Create a space for a continuum depicting 1 to 10, with 1 being very low to 10 being very high (I always say that it's up to individuals to decide what very low or very high may look like for

themselves). Then ask them to move to where they would rate their team/organisation on a question such as 'How inclusive is your organisation?' or 'How effective is your organisation when working across cultures?'

This can open up rich discussions at the start of a session about how the participants view their current situation. As with all exercises, think about context and who is in the room in terms of whether people would be OK about indicating what they think about how well their organisation is doing.

3. Ask the group to perform a simple task, then ask them to redo it but differently. For example, you may ask people to fold their arms then ask them to refold them but with the opposite arm on top. Then ask people how that felt for them. Often people will share that it felt weird, or unnatural, or they had to really think about it. Change is often uncomfortable to start with. You may also have people in the group who have great body symmetry and didn't feel any difference. And so it is with working with difference; for some it can be uncomfortable and for others they are barely noticing that they are making an adaptation from their norm, or they have many norms.

There are different thoughts you can pull from an exercise such as this around how difficult it is to make even small changes or how we can start to recognise feelings of discomfort that can arise when people act and think differently from our norms and how we can become comfortable with this discomfort in order to be culturally intelligent.

Any of these three simple exercises can be useful at the start of a training and can be adapted for large or small groups whether in person, hybrid or virtual. The benefit of using movement is that everyone is communicating whether they speak or not, through the position they take. It also creates a visual that works well for some.

A couple of interviewees mentioned psychological safety, or spoke to practices that would foster it, within their response to this question, and most mentioned it during the interview. I will return to the important subject of psychological safety in Chapter 5 on CQ Drive, so at this point I'll just say that, at the start of training, accepting the words and narratives people share without judgement is important. It's typically not the time to be questioning, disagreeing or interrupting.

What's important is that your participants can relax into the learning. Know your introduction and speak with confidence (whether you feel it or not), as your participants will be feeding off all the cues you give and you want them to know they are in good hands. If you are going to wing any part of your training sessions, my suggestion would be not to make it the opening! David said that the first five to 15 minutes was probably the part he obsesses over the most. It's good advice!

The feedback I received from people who read early drafts of this book was that they wanted to know when to start with purpose, or human connection, or the concept. This is for you to decide. I'm aware that since the interviews, I've experimented more (even with throwing out a question like Andrej does, and being pleasantly surprised by the response!).

Do your research about the context you are going into. Know the purpose you have and be prepared to try different things. Sometimes it can be useful to be countercultural and then explore this later in the session. And remember, there are often people who are resistant in any room. Experience has taught me that yes, the start is important, but there are lots of opportunities to connect during any training session.

Key takeaways

✧ Plan and practise how you are going to open any training session.

✧ Plan what aspects of purpose, human connection and key concepts you are going to lead with and use as the theme to engage your participants.

✧ Take steps to engage participants' imagination from the start, to help people feel something different, contribute their thoughts and connect with their purpose.

✧ We are always communicating (whether we're speaking or not), so how we listen and receive information from participants is as important as what we say (if not more so).

✧ Remember to accept people as they are; some people (or groups) will be more resistant, sceptical or preoccupied than others.

Questions to consider

✧ What impact do you want the start of your training sessions to have on your participants?

✧ What would you share to hook them in on the theme of purpose? To hook them in on the theme of human connection? To hook them in on concepts? Are you prepared to experiment?

✧ Do you have a standard approach to starting? Do you mix it up? What is your reasoning for that?

✧ How do you enable your participants to share thoughts or to feel something quickly at the start of sessions?

Chapter 4

Cultural value preferences

Once you see culture, you can't unsee it. Where we don't understand culture, we judge, and we usually judge negatively. And because we judge negatively, we cannot meet halfway.
– Catherine Wu

Throughout the interviews, everyone mentioned cultural values, both in terms of how they included the topic within their training but also how, as a trainer, they had to recognise their own cultural values and how they impacted on their preferences during training.

The purpose of this chapter is to encourage you to think about how you share the concept of cultural values with your participants and to reflect on how culture has shaped your behavioural preferences and how these impact your training. There has been much research around the world by academics about how our cultures shape our behavioural preferences and the unspoken values that can sit behind our actions and ways of doing.[7]

The groups we have been part of in our lives will have shaped how we perceive the behaviours of others. What do we consider

---

7 Authors, or reports, to search for to build your knowledge of cultural values include Hofstede, Inglehart, Schwartz, GLOBE (Global Leadership and Organizational Behavior Effectiveness), Minko and Trompenaars. It is worth noting that different academics conceptualise cultural values differently. A useful research paper about this is Maleki & de Jong 2014.

is good, bad, polite or friendly? Much of the way in which we do things is taught to us when we are young and we forget we ever learned why we have preferences and biases for doing this a particular way, or what those preferences suggest about what is valued. Cultural value dimensions is a concept that means we can have a preference along multiple continuums that includes such things as how we identify with a group, or power, or feel about how direct or expressive we should be in communication. These preferences have been shaped by the cultures we have been part of.

I sometimes describe the concept of cultural value dimensions by saying, 'Imagine you have been asked to work in a room and you can choose its shade, from the very palest of pinks to the deepest of scarlets. There may be a shade you know would be your preference, or you may not care as you would be fine with any of the shades, or you may be aware that to be surrounded all day by a certain shade would make you uncomfortable or even prevent you from being able to concentrate and focus.'

Cultural values are about differences and preferences that sometimes barely impact us and sometimes throw us off being able to relate effectively. What all the interviewees spoke about was how discussing these cultural values enabled people to recognise the impact of culture in their situation. One of the key findings of the research into what makes a person culturally intelligent is that 'the culturally intelligent have a good grasp of overarching patterns that exist across various cultures' (Livermore 2013).

Cultural values and your training

Jennifer said that she enters any training room having done her research, so she has a picture of what she thinks she is coming into, but it's a draft in her mind and she is constantly updating that draft. The interviewees spoke about how they were intentional about noticing how culture and behaviours were impacting the space. This started from the point at which people came into the room.

- Did people say hello?
- What information did participants think was important to share with you in those introductions?
- How are participants interacting with each other?
- What impact is that having on you?

Being observant enables you to build a picture of which cultural values could be important to your participants. (This is much harder in a virtual set-up where there is less visible interaction going on between people.)

Culture is complex. The cultural dimensions enable you to bring some clarity to what can feel vague and abstract, and when you notice behavioural differences you can choose not to judge but to consider different perspectives and values that may be at play.

Here are a few points that are always worth reminding yourself and participants of:

- This is about preference. There is no better or worse place to be. However, you may feel that there is a better and worse place to be. That provides an opportunity to reflect on what that tells you about yourself and how cultures have shaped you.
- There is no preference about a cultural value that makes you more adaptable than others. It is just your preference. I often hear people describe themselves as a balanced, neutral or adaptable person who doesn't have a strong preference for either side of a cultural value dimension. It just means that is your preference, not that you are more adaptable.
- While having an understanding of cultural values gives us an awareness of what could be going on, it is not a shortcut to complete stories. People and situations are complex. There are typically many contributing factors.
- Early research was about national differences. There is frequently as much diversity within a group as there is between groups; it is about averages and likelihood. And the larger the group, the more diversity there is. The chances of me ever fully knowing all the cultural differences that exist within Glasgow,

the city where I live, is small, but I can make generalisations to be held lightly and reframed. What is familiar and expected within this group?

- How you think about your individual cultural values will also be relative to whatever reference point you have in mind when thinking about them (or when completing the CQ assessment, which includes ten behavioural preferences). Preferences can change when viewed from a different perspective, or when we move context or have new experiences.

- Recognising your own preferences and the preferences of others is key.

A concern sometimes shared by participants is that thinking in terms of cultural values can create stereotypes. A couple of the interviewees who delivered in many geographies and settings spoke about how they found that there was often a concern about stereotypes in the West, and perhaps more of a reliance and desire for them when working in the East, with one interviewee saying he tends to give more time for this discussion when working in Asia. I have found that in many settings, including UK academic ones, I've had people express disappointment that there is not just an easy rule that can be applied to all people in a group. Cultural values are not rules – they are possibilities and opportunities to explore and apply your CQ.

Another concern raised was that there was sometimes confusion about the connection between cultural values and CQ. Understanding the values and how they shape behaviours is building your cultural awareness, your CQ Knowledge. Having knowledge contributes but is not enough to make you culturally intelligent.

Keep emphasising that knowing about different behavioural preferences, shaped by cultural values, gives us the opportunity to apply CQ. There is no universal way of describing cultural values; the terms and descriptors are used differently by different academics. It is a separate body of work to the research on cultural intelligence. CQ is the capability to navigate the differences in our ways of thinking about and behaving in our worlds.

In your planning, think about which cultural value concepts it would be most useful to include in your training. Many of the interviewees spoke about how, following their discussions with the client, they may introduce three or four cultural value concepts and explore in depth how they were showing up.

When I'm working to develop CQ trainers, I'll talk to the ten that are included in the Cultural Intelligence Center's CQ assessment feedback reports so that they have an understanding and can then select what is most useful in their contexts.

When sharing information about cultural values and behavioural preferences, ensure you share examples that are relevant to your audience and the purpose of the training. If left at a high-level description, it can sometimes feel abstract and distant. Pull from your talks with clients and your knowledge of how culture shows up in the context your participants are in to share examples and stories your participants will recognise and be familiar with. Better still, encourage your audience to share and discuss how different cultural values show up for them.

All the interviewees spoke about how power dynamics can impact training. Many of them also mentioned how preference for individualism or collectivism (identifying more with individual goals and rights or group ones) can show up in a training. Therefore I'm going to include some thoughts on both these cultural values, along with how we describe and recognise our preference for the dimension described as 'being/doing' in the CQ feedback reports from the Cultural Intelligence Center, because in my work with newly CQ certified facilitators, this is the one that I most often hear misunderstood.

This is not a book about cultural values, which is why I've selected just a few to speak to.

How would you have made that selection?

How do you identify with the group? Individualism and collectivism

* Were you brought up in a group that favoured words such as 'I' and 'mine' or 'we' and 'ours'?
* What do you most value, independence or interdependence?
* When there is a difference of opinion, do you favour speaking up and sharing your point of view (even if you know it may create discord), or is your preference for preserving harmony in the group?

Each of these questions may give you an indication of your preference for placing an emphasis on individual goals and rights versus group goals and the relationships within that group. You might also be aware that in different groups your preference may change.

Justin shared that earlier in his career he had been working in Rwanda with an American company. He would often receive the invitation, 'Do you want to join us for lunch?' He would decline. His understanding was that they were not saying, 'We want you to join us for lunch.' The emphasis was on him as an individual to say he wanted to come, which did not feel right for him. Justin said that while he was speaking in English, the language he spoke and heard and the language he meant were different things, because he actually would have liked to join these colleagues for lunch.

Buhle wrote the following in a LinkedIn post:

Ubuntu is an African philosophy or concept of humanity. It has guided us Africans to always be community or 'other-minded' in our daily dealings. In essence a person's humanity is tied to others around them. In African languages like isiZulu and SeSotho, Ubuntu is 'Umuntu wumuntu ngabantu' *(Zulu) or* 'Motho ke motho ka batho' *(Sotho), directly translated as, 'A person is a person through other people.' In English, this is commonly translated as 'I am because you are' or 'I am* *because we are'. Both of these are an attempt at making this concept easy to understand for people with a different mindset or cultural value orientation. In the original language of Ubuntu, the individual speaking (I) is not the centre; it simply says, 'a person or a human' (**umuntu** or **motho**).*

This is a classic case of lost in translation. In making the concept understandable to a different culture, it kind of loses its original meaning. Explaining Ubuntu by putting yourself at the centre kind of misses the point altogether. Ubuntu basically says, I'm not the centre, but we are! It encourages us to think of the good for the people as opposed to focusing on what's good for me and mine. (Dlamini 2024)

Each time I've taken the CQ assessment, my feedback reports indicate I have a strong preference for collectivism. When Buhle and Justin share stories of what it is to be collectivist from their perspective, they immediately make me realise that if I shift my frame of reference away from my context, I would no longer think of myself as having such a strong collectivist preference.

Two people who have taken the CQ assessment and are seeing a similar descriptor for their cultural value preference may have very different reference points. Don't assume sameness; explore meanings from different perspectives.

I can recall several instances in my work history where the preference for 'me' or 'we' has had an impact. I led on a leadership development programme over three years with the British Council, which we piloted first with participants from Scotland, Jordan and Egypt, with the trainers coming from Jordan, Egypt and the UK. The pedagogical approaches were rooted in appreciative inquiry, systems thinking and Ubuntu.

Buhle is right. Ubuntu was translated for our Western audience as 'I am, because you are, because we are'. The different focus on 'I' and 'we' showed up quickly with the training design team. The UK trainers wanted to emphasise developing 'me' (with the rationale being that it is only 'me' I have agency over). The trainers from Jordan and Egypt wanted to focus on 'we' (with the rationale being that being human is to be connected and interconnected; we are nothing without each other). The decision was made to speak to both as we could not resolve that one should have preference over the other.

This tension around a preference for 'me' or 'we' shows up in so many areas of work in how we motivate, reward and develop people. For example, do you have a recognition scheme for individual or team performance? It can impact key processes such as recruitment. I recall, with a degree of shame, when interviewing at the British Council, that candidates who spoke to 'we' rather than 'I' were judged as being unable to articulate their individual contribution and as such were always marked down. There was never any notion or awareness that culture, and therefore cultural values, were relevant and playing a part in our decision making.

It's a story I often share when I'm providing CQ training to support inclusion in the UK. It's a story that often leads to people sharing their stories. When working with a group of leaders in an NHS Trust, they shared that they had interviewed people for a senior nursing role. There had been a person acting in the role for a while before the substantive post was advertised. This person was excellent and clearly having a positive impact in the role. However, during the interview, the candidate spoke with a preference for 'we'. Another candidate (who wasn't known to the recruitment panel) spoke with a preference for 'I'. As this reflected the cultural preference of the recruitment panel, it gave that candidate an edge, as the answers that spoke to the achievement of 'we' were not considered to have as much merit.

They told me the appointment was a disaster and created all sorts of extra issues, not least because the candidate recruited was a white woman and the senior nurse who had already proven their capability in the role was a black woman. This hidden element of how culture can show up contributes to decisions that damage trust and inclusion in organisations and in this case created an optic that served to reinforce an impression of racism in decision making.

What experiences and stories can you share about individualism and collectivism preferences and how they relate to your area of purpose, whether it is relocation, leadership, international team effectiveness or inclusion?

As a trainer, you want to know your own preferences for 'me' or 'we', as it has an impact on many aspects of training. Will the language of 'I' or 'we' best motivate and engage your participants? Will participants speak out as individuals or will small group discussions and reporting back on behalf of a group be a better fit? Do you adjust when you spot the clues?

Hierarchy: how comfortable are you with differences in power?

- Were you encouraged to question or disagree with parents and teachers?
- Do you prefer there to be a very clear chain of command in the groups you are part of?
- Can you learn something useful from everyone?

How you responded to these questions may give you an indication as to what your relationship with power and status may be. The dominant norm around the world is for there to be a top-down, hierarchical approach to leadership (known as 'high power difference' in CQ assessments).

My home country, Scotland, has a day in the year to celebrate the life and works of a poet, Robert (or Rabbie) Burns, who died in 1796. One of the themes in his poetry is the equality of humanity. When our Parliament reopened in 1999 after an absence of 292 years, one of his most famous poems, 'A Man's a Man for a' That', was read out. It speaks to the equality of everyone. Without a doubt, the mantra that I'm no better than anyone else is strong in me, as is the other half of that maxim – that I'm not less than anyone either.

I go into training sessions with the mindset that I'm an equal to everyone – not in the sense of status (I'm often the person with least rank and status in the space), but in the sense that my typical perspective is that everyone in the room has equal worth and I'm there for a purpose, and that requires me to question and to reflect back (even, sometimes especially, when that may be a difficult reflection for someone to receive). My preference is to hear every voice, or have every voice contribute somehow, and each voice has the same importance to me. It can be both a strength and my Achilles' heel. While my norm may be to treat every voice as having equal weight, it isn't always the norm, expectation or even what works best in the space.

When I'm working internationally, or at a one-off event, I typically find it easier to adapt and pay more attention to my preferences and expectations around showing respect or deference and engaging with different people within a hierarchy, but when I have a long-term relationship with clients or partners, I can relax into not paying as much attention to this preference as I should. When I lose work or get negative feedback (which thankfully is rare), reflection often leads back to me not observing hierarchy enough for the traditions and liking of the people I was with.

Andrej says that, near the start of training sessions, he tells participants that he is going to challenge them and ask uncomfortable questions. He also asks to be challenged and says, 'It's OK. When I challenge you, I'm not disrespecting your authority. I acknowledge your position in this organisation. But to make this relationship during this programme effective and sustainable, it needs to be equal.'

How do you think of your relationship with the people you train? What do words such as equality, status, hierarchy mean to you when training? It's no surprise to me that of all the different ways in which culture shapes our preferences, it was hierarchy in the training room that was spoken about the most during the interviews.

It's not just your expectations and preferences about hierarchy that you take into training; you work in spaces where you may, or may not, be aware of the hierarchies and attitudes to it within the room. Knowing and not knowing have different challenges and advantages. What kinds of groups you work with, in what type of organisation and where in the world will have a big impact on how hierarchy shows up during your training programmes. Some of the interviewees felt that the shift to hosting more virtual training, which has sped up since the Covid-19 pandemic, had amplified how hierarchy can sometimes play out in training spaces. They spoke about strategies they used when hierarchy was having the impact of preventing discussions, which they all felt were necessary for successful CQ training. This sometimes involved thinking about the groupings that people are in for discussions (ideally in advance, but it may be that you have to react to the room and start mixing groups around as you respond to dynamics).

Fenny, who trains a lot in Asia, spoke about often being too ambitious when she first started training in wanting to mix junior staff with their supervisors in the hope that they would open up and present ideas in the moment to the boss. With experience, her view is that this was often the wrong strategy. When she is in a high power difference context, what typically works better is creating discussion groups by role/level and then in the debrief people get to see the difference in thought, and how the different lens and perspectives lead to a different focus and ideas – ideally with the takeaway being that these different perspectives can be captured and used in development (be that product or policy) without trying to make people operate outside their cultural values during the discussions.

Many of the interviewees, wherever their location, had experience of a boss who insists on joining to see how everyone engages with the training, whose presence stops people from speaking and exploring freely, or who speaks first then everyone agrees with them, or where no one will speak until they do. Suggestions on how to approach a boss and tell them that their presence might be limiting the sharing of ideas included raising your authority in the room to delay input from the dominant person, quietly taking the boss into your confidence and showing respect and/or flattery to try to either encourage them to delay their responses or privately suggesting the best thing they could do would be to leave the training during a break (there was never a suggestion that this should be said publicly).

Another approach was to give time for individual reflection and ask people to write something on the topic before going into group discussions. You can then encourage a round of sharing reflections within each group to start the discussion. This way, everyone will have thought about the question whether they speak or not, and an opportunity for sharing those thoughts has been created. There is rarely a right or wrong way, but there may be a better or worse way in the context you are in.

I frequently deliver sessions across teams, departments or services where there is a mix in status and position in the room, and it is a positive aspect in terms of the training and the impact it can have. No one suggested that you should not have training with teams where a boss is present; it was more about developing your knowledge in advance as to what impact this may have and having strategies you can use to ensure your training achieves its aims.

As well as how you respond to hierarchy in your training, you also want to encourage participants to share how they see this showing up. I've heard participants who work in organisations where the authority to make decisions is devolved talk about peers lacking in confidence because they operate in different contexts where getting the agreement of the boss is the way to get things done. In my experience, this has arisen most often with UK organisations that work with organisations in the Gulf or China. Frustration is expressed by colleagues in the UK who have authority delegated to them that agreement cannot be reached within a meeting of peers from the different nations. Understanding what needs to happen for both sides to reach agreement, and doing so in the best way for their particular context, enables time to be built into thinking and planning and reduces judgement and anxiety.

I remember working with a team in the north of England when, following an exploration of their relationship with hierarchy, the leader reflected back to me that she constantly felt she was 'banging her head against the wall'. (This is a metaphor used in the UK that speaks to the frustration of repeatedly trying, or asking for, something and being unable to change the situation.) The leader was the only person in the team with a preference for low power distance and was always trying to engage the team in discussions about strategy, for instance. The team resisted as, for them, those were choices for the leadership to make.

Do you see this showing up in your training? Individuals or groups may want to have some control, or at least some discussion, over the agenda or activities. It may be one person; it may be a group. That, combined with aspects such as your aim, your responses and preferences around hierarchy and the time available, may all impact on how you respond. Know your preference and how different responses to hierarchy within a training context may impact you, so that you can develop a toolkit of potential responses.

Being/doing: prioritising, scheduling and relationship with time and people

This cultural value dimension is connected to how we feel productive and go about getting things done. A possible indicator for this is whether you work to live, or live to work. Do you have a preference for unstructured time (knowing that life will bring things to you), or do you like to plan a structure of how you will use time? Are you able to 'be' in the moment or are you pitching towards what you will be 'doing' next?

In different contexts, from mentoring and training CQ trainers to conversations with people who talk about what they include or exclude from their development programmes, this is a cultural value that I'm aware is often dismissed or spoken about as though it has no impact in the world of work. We take the influences from our cultures with us everywhere.

When training trainers in CQ, I have heard people say that this is about achievement. People achieve regardless of their preference. Likewise, I've heard the description that groups that are more 'being' orientated can approach life passively and suspect this description comes from someone who is more 'doing' orientated. There are choices attached to where you focus and if a person focuses their energy on the person in front of them (rather than the person they were scheduled to see), or prioritises family, social or religious obligations over work deadlines, that isn't about being passive, it's about making a choice about what is important.

I worked with a mentee who, once we had discussed this cultural value in more depth, said that rather than dismissing it, he was seeing it everywhere – from a colleague who was furious about the 'disrespect' shown by someone sending a WhatsApp message about work after working hours (which was normal in the part of the world the person was sending the message from, which my mentee knew well), to rethinking discussions about expectations of deadlines set for a team in Saudi Arabia during Ramadan.

Your approach to how you schedule and think about structuring activities can impact on whether you feel productive, and it can also impact on whether you feel heard, respected or taken advantage of. I see the judgements and stress that can come from not having thought about this value in both international and local organisations. For themes around building trust, hybrid working, wellbeing and inclusion, it can be a very useful value and preference to explore.

It also shows up during training. A few of the interviewees spoke about how they were very 'doing' orientated when they started training – thinking about how much time was to be spent on each aspect of the training, which activities, for how long, and perhaps panicking when they spent longer than they meant to on a particular area and then getting caught up in what they were meant to 'do'. All of this detracted from focusing their energy outward so they could 'be' in the room, honing their ability to feel the energy or mood and respond to it.

When someone asks a question, are you prepared to 'be' where the question takes you, even if it strays from your schedule and plan? Some trainers prefer to use phrases such as 'I'll get back to you after the training' so that the schedule isn't disrupted. Some of the interviewees were very much of the view that plans were there to be ripped up, depending on where the participants needed to 'be'.

Thinking of cultural values

If you are thinking that some of the ways in which culture shapes our behavioural preferences aren't relevant to work, international effectiveness, inclusion, change or training, or you only have a sentence of high-level thought about them, take some time to explore, to be actively curious about it so that you can keep deepening your knowledge and relate it to your purpose.

It doesn't mean that you have to introduce each value preference into each training programme (people can only absorb so much information), but it does build your capacity to notice patterns that may show up in a room or discussion. Having taken time to explore, notice and build awareness of your preferences and experiences of them will help you to share the information through examples and stories when it's useful for the groups you're working with.

I sometimes hear people give reasoning, rooted in one cultural value, as to why participants are behaving a certain way, such as not speaking. Unless you have the space to explore in depth what lies behind a behaviour, you don't know the reason. We are complex beings and typically many factors contribute to how we act. There can be lots of reasons why people don't speak up during a training. Cultural values such as not speaking before the boss, or expectations of the trainer to provide all the learning, or a fear of being wrong, may be part of the reason, as could a lack of sleep, introversion or just not being bothered about the topic.

As a trainer, you want to use your knowledge of cultural values to plan for behavioural preferences that may be dominant in the groups you work with, while having options that you can adapt to if you find that your training plan isn't working – all the while keeping a curious, open mindset as to what is impacting you and others.

When working with groups, a common response to exploring

how the values of our cultures shape behavioural preferences is that people who are put together due to an aspect of their identities get to explore layers of diversity within their group. An important message from the work of the Cultural Intelligence Center is that all groups have diversity. How do you look out for, notice and acknowledge that?

Another response often mentioned during the interviews was that if groups decide that a particular preference is the best one, the conversation moves towards how to get everyone to value being direct or have a preference for low power difference or similar. The aim is to include different values, approaches and behaviours to reach the shared goal.

As Buhle said, the message is not that you need to change who you are. The message is that if you understand that there are these differences and the impact that they have in the way you work with others, then you have options to mitigate against some of the challenges.

I also hear trainers say that this is the information and content people love, so they focus on this. Who doesn't like to discover things about themselves while exploring how cultural values can shape our behavioural preferences? As a trainer, spending time where there is no right or wrong, just difference, is also comfortable. However, these differences present the opportunity to use your CQ. The capabilities of cultural intelligence enable you to work and relate well to diversity. The CQ research shows that each of the capabilities is important, so if you only focus on building your knowledge, you won't enhance the capability of people to be more effective and inclusive in culturally diverse contexts. Keep building your knowledge and doing that inner work as more awareness creates more choices about the responses you have, and those choices impact on outcomes.

Key takeaways

✧ If you are in the field of CQ training, you have inner work to do. Take time to really understand how culture has shaped you and your approaches to life, relationships, work and training.

✧ When you hear judgements, ask people to describe just the behaviour and then reframe what they are experiencing using the language of cultural values and behavioural preferences. (Notice this in yourself, too.)

✧ In your training programmes, plan for what preferences may be most important for the theme. Decide whether being broader or deeper is more useful for the purpose and time available.

✧ Not everything is about culture. What else is going on? This is a useful question to ask.

✧ Take time to reflect after a training and describe groups you have worked with. Which language do you find yourself gravitating towards? Keep building the habit of seeing culture.

Questions to consider

✧ What is your ideal training session? How have your cultural experiences shaped this ideal? What does it tell you of your cultural preferences?

✧ When have you been most comfortable/uncomfortable when delivering a training? What can you learn about yourself and your cultural preferences from your responses?

✧ What are the key takeaways you want for your participants when you explore cultural values and behavioural preferences with them?

Chapter 5

Developing CQ Drive

L'appétit vient en mangeant. (French proverb: 'The appetite comes with eating.') – Justin Ngoga

What's your motivation to even want to effectively relate to and work across cultures? This is the question that sits at the heart of developing CQ Drive, the capability that focuses on building our motivation and confidence to work well where there is cultural difference, whatever that cultural difference may be.

When I first took a CQ assessment back in 2013, I assumed CQ Drive would be my strongest capability. I had loved my career with the British Council, working with colleagues and students from around the world, and when I started my own business in 2010, I wanted to keep meeting and working with people from many places. When I received my report, my CQ Drive feedback was so-so and far from being my strongest capability. It gave me pause for reflection. I found myself asking why I'd been to France a few times but never eaten snails – a dish that the French are known for but you don't see in the UK. I wondered how much this spoke to a desire not to stray too far from my comfort zone. I have now eaten snails (delicious) and more generally I have become braver about doing and trying things that for whatever reason I think I may not like.

I also found myself asking an uncomfortable question. Do I only like diversity when it's kind of like me? 'Like me' can be many things. It could be the woman in the room, the Scottish voice in the room, the age group, the profession, the parent and so on.

I loved working with international students from across the globe as their perspectives often enabled me to see my world differently. For example, being brought up in north-east Scotland, it was a generally held 'truth' that our weather was fairly rubbish (a belief that seems to be shared across the UK). Imagine my surprise when a student from Colombia told me how lucky I was with the weather in Scotland. He suggested that this was why there were so many inventions from Scotland, as we were always having to adapt to a different weather environment, whereas in Bogotá the weather is fairly consistent and you have to make a journey to be in a different weather environment.

I heard this but didn't really absorb it until I heard the same comment about how lucky we were with our weather from a man from Bahrain. Over time, hearing about how lucky I was with the weather in Scotland and how the constant changes suggested the case for inventiveness has changed my perspective (and it is true that you can experience many seasons of weather in one hour). Rather than being downbeat about the weather in my country, I find that I now have a more optimistic disposition, wondering if today will be the day when I invent something. However, I'm unaware if there is a link between weather variability and inventiveness and, to date, while my mood is optimistic, I've not invented anything!

I love speaking with people and hearing different perspectives that challenge aspects of my world view. This speaks to my intrinsic interest in finding joy in engaging with people from different places, different religions, different age groups... just difference. However, the CQ Drive capability isn't only about the enjoyment; it's also about the drive to be persistent and overcome the challenges that working with diversity can bring.

When I pondered that question, 'Do I only like diversity when it is kind of like me?', I reflected that my network was skewed towards people from the education and public sectors and I could be quite uncomfortable in a business-focused, entrepreneurial group where it could sometimes seem to me that people were driven by values that didn't resonate with me. Likewise with politics. Engaging with people and groups with very different political outlooks from me could at times be a real challenge, even to want to stay in the conversation and keep being civil!

Engaging your CQ Drive

A few interviewees said that it was at the point of being invited to work with certain clients that they would feel a reaction as they thought, 'Do I even want to work with these people?' Connecting with the reaction you are having to working with any group of people is important. What does it tell you about your CQ Drive?

Feeling that lack of motivation, the CQ Drive, to even start working with some groups was expressed in different ways during the interviews. Some interviewees shared that their confidence had been knocked during previous work with certain groups, or sensed that their personal values didn't align with the client's intentions. Some felt that the invitation to provide training was just part of a tick-box exercise rather than a commitment to enhance team dynamics or inclusion, or that it wouldn't truly address the client's challenges, or that the purpose of the organisation was at odds with enhancing their CQ Drive.

CQ Drive can ebb and flow. Think about your purpose and why you do the work you do. Recognise that a dip in your CQ Drive can be related to a disconnect between the work and what is important to you.

- What impacts your CQ Drive in a positive or negative way?
- Is it important for you to engage and build your CQ Drive for certain types of work?

In 2017, I was invited to Pakistan to provide CQ training to various businesses by the International Business Council in Karachi. It was the first international trip I had taken for work, which most people who shared their opinion with me were negative about. People I barely knew gave opinions on what kind of person (or mother) I must be to travel to a country that they deemed unsafe. Even my friends of Pakistani heritage gave me advice about risks, such as to ensure I didn't buy water from street vendors. Uncharacteristically, my dad and husband were quiet, which spoke volumes in itself about their concern.

However, I had great faith in my host, Hammad Amjad, whom I had first met in Glasgow when I was giving a presentation on CQ for businesses. The work had taken a while to come to fruition and I was able to speak with many different people who had lived and worked in Karachi. What was impacting on my confidence, part of my CQ Drive, was not about place; it was the knowledge that one of the groups I would be working with were senior executives from UBL Bank. I had never worked with bankers!

This speaks to my earlier assessment of areas where my CQ Drive can be impacted, and I can feel that sense of my confidence being questioned in different business sectors. I'm unclear as to why it is sector, rather than place, which has that impact. I'd love to give a good insight on that. However, regardless of my confidence about being among executives from a business I knew nothing about, it did not stop me travelling and having a great time working with different business groups in Karachi.

Paying attention to your CQ Drive

There are three sub-dimensions to CQ Drive. As well as sharing them, through questions, storytelling and insights with your participants, also take time to reflect on them all as a trainer in this field.

1. **Intrinsic interests:** What gives you a sense of joy, satisfaction and pride about doing your CQ training work? Does this vary depending on the profession and management level of the participants, or the place or purpose of the training?
2. **Extrinsic interests:** What are the benefits for you as a trainer? Does it build your credibility? Your capabilities as a CQ trainer? Your reputation? Your income or standing in your organisation?

3. **Self-efficacy:** How confident are you feeling about working with any particular group of people and the purpose of working with them?

Catherine said, 'Drive is knowing that, in spite of the challenges, you can get things done, you will overcome, you will succeed. And actually, that element of drive is built over time through repeated experiences.'

I have certainly found that to be true regarding building my confidence in working with people, regardless of the sector they are from. Opportunities have presented themselves that have enabled me to work with professionals in organisations as diverse as oil and gas companies, supermarkets and hospitals, holding the belief that I have expertise in cultural intelligence and as a trainer, and my participants have the expertise in their work – and the magic happens when these are brought together. You need to encourage the people you are working with to be persistent and remind yourself of that.

When asking the interviewees which capability they found hardest to develop, CQ Drive was in joint second place with three saying this was the capability that they have struggled with. The challenges were expressed in different ways. For some it was about recognising that working with different groups could lead to overthinking and worrying about their 'fit' in specific scenarios or having a dislike of certain aspects of their working life such as networking, and these reflections made them realise that there was always work to do with developing and engaging their CQ Drive. A couple of interviewees also shared that, while CQ Drive was high in most working contexts, outside work that could be less so. For example, they shared that they did not have high CQ Drive on holiday and wanted to stay inside their comfort zone in order to relax.

It is worth noting that some research has found a link between high levels of extroversion and CQ Drive (Ang et al 2006), so taking time to think about when you feel more or less introverted or extroverted could also be a useful reflection.

What was also discussed, both from the perspective of living in specific societies and being in some work contexts, was the exhaustion some interviewees felt when the values and actions of everyone around them were not only different, but different in ways that undermined their personal sense of worth or deeply held morals about what was felt to be right and wrong.

All the interviewees have high cultural intelligence, but sometimes, as one suggested, it is not about CQ – it is about self-compassion. CQ isn't mandatory, or perhaps even for the best sometimes. (This thought will be returned to in Chapter 12 under the question, 'What is the culturally intelligent way to deal with profound ethical differences?')

There is a need for you to check in with yourself and what is happening around you. As a trainer, you need to hold that, within a group with whom you are working, there are many reasons why someone may not be motivated to engage with CQ or have the energy to invest in their CQ Drive. While you may be thinking of your training as happening in a specific location, participants could be connected to and impacted by events happening anywhere in the world.

Creating an environment conducive to engaging CQ Drive

In your training, you want to enable your participants to be able to reflect on and think about how they can build their CQ Drive. There are at least three things that contribute to creating a positive environment for people to be encouraged to develop and use their CQ. These are the same in an organisation as they are in your training. They are psychological safety, vision and wellbeing.

1. Psychological safety

Andrej said that we don't learn at a cognitive level – we learn at an emotional level. Rational thinking comes later. So, as a trainer, you need to be able to create a space in which people generate insight. To share insights, you need to feel safe. Nearly all the interviewees mentioned the importance of psychological safety.

There are so many layers to this, including giving clear expectations around timings and involvement, asking people to share the name they would like to be called by, and taking time to explore which behaviours people would like to see from you and from each other. Samara shared how important it is to be curious about what people mean by the words they use. For example, someone might say that they want everyone to be treated with respect or for information shared to be treated as confidential.

- What does being treated with respect look like to you?
- What do you mean by confidential?

Taking the time to be curious and explore enables a number of things. It shows that you are not just going to be surface level. You are demonstrating that you are interested in understanding and will take the time to reach an outcome for the group (which may not always be easy). It opens up space for others to state how they understand the word. Sometimes this can be a lengthy process, particularly if there have been tensions in the group of people with whom you are working. Throughout, ideally you will use the words you have been given, rather than edit in your preferences for the meanings.

Taking time to create an agreement on behaviours helps to establish open, transparent and respectful communication. If you are training in person, you can have these behaviour guidelines captured and on display. If you are online, take notes and refer back to them when useful. If you are meeting on multiple occasions with the same group, it is worth revisiting and checking in to see if they want to add or change anything.

Many of the interviewees, in all regions of the world, spoke about using stories to help create a psychologically safe space, particularly stories about themselves and their journey with CQ. In Jennifer's words, 'Be intentional in allowing your audience to connect with you. This means that your audience needs to connect with you as an individual behind all the things you're trying to tell them or teach them. Because there's a danger that when you hold yourself back, you may be saying intelligent stuff, but you are quite remote. They don't get to know you. They don't get to connect with you, and as human beings we connect with people. And we feel safer with people we trust, and we trust people more when we can connect with who they are.'

A note of caution. The interviewees who worked in Asia and the West spoke about how a certain type of charisma was valued in the West and less so in the Asian countries they worked in, or they had encountered the recommendation to be vulnerable in the West and again to be careful how and when in a training session this was displayed in Asia.

This is true about working in different sectors, too. For example, in academia, too much focus on a personal story without the data to back up why it is relevant to the goal of the session can create a barrier. Think about the stories you are going to share, relate them to the context of the people you are working with and be clear about why you are sharing them. If they are not linked to a learning point, sharing experiences can come across as offloading or boasting. And remember, you want your participants to share their thoughts and stories more than you share your own.

We can learn lessons about CQ from all aspects of our lives, but it is always up to you what you share. Do you feel secure and safe sharing this aspect of your experience? Does it serve a learning purpose? If not, what else could you speak to?

One of the interviewees' most cited approaches to use alongside CQ was the change management work of John Kotter. He speaks to the need to engage head and heart for getting buy-in to change agendas. As a trainer, you are hoping that your participants will commit to changes, and for that to happen there is a need for data to speak to the head and stories to speak to the heart. Sandra said that in her work supporting DEI, an issue she may be speaking about is the attrition rate of people of colour within an organisation, who may be joining then leaving as though there is a revolving door in perpetual motion. Getting the hard data is not the difficult part. Thinking through the stories that can be shared to influence buy-in is the important 'heart' piece. As Sandra said, the incredible role of storytelling and perspective-taking can absolutely influence buy-in. What is useful for people to take away is how useful storytelling is at all levels throughout their organisation.

Creating a psychologically safe space is about being intentional from start to finish. Create the habit of checking in with yourself to notice how you are feeling, as whether you are feeling interested, irritated or anxious will impact on how you respond to others. If you are aiming to create the space for your participants to generate insight, then you need to be demonstrating calm (whether you feel it or not).

More than one of the interviewees quoted a line attributed to Maya Angelou: 'I've learned that people will forget what you said, people will forget what you did, but people will never forget how you made them feel.' Be intentional about creating an environment where people feel their words are heard, that their thoughts and experience matter and that they get a sense of who you are as a trainer.

2. Vision

It is most impactful when people generate their own vision about becoming more culturally intelligent, be that individually, as a team or across their organisation. Where relevant, make clear links, or invite participants to do so, between the development of CQ and achieving the organisation's vision.

In Chapter 1, you read about the benefits of developing CQ, which research has demonstrated in multiple contexts around the world. As a trainer, weave discussions about the relevant proven benefits into discussions about the vision that the organisation is working towards and the training can contribute to.

When I am hosting open learning days or asking participants at organisational events in the UK what their motivation is for participating in the training, one of the most common responses I hear at an individual level is, 'I don't want to offend anyone.' I hear this so often that I realise it is a cultural trait in the UK. This motivation is rooted in avoiding something.

At an organisational level, training can sometimes be prompted because of negative events and again this can lead to motivation being expressed as the desire to avoid something (such as poor customer reviews, a failing merger or staff disciplinary procedures). It is important to understand the pain points – however, it is not a vision.

In the same way as when you're establishing which behaviours would contribute to a positive learning environment by questioning words such as respect or confidential, again it is useful to question people when they express motivation in terms of what they want to avoid – not to dismiss it but to add to it by asking questions that will enable someone to think about what they are working towards in positive terms.

- If you don't want to offend anyone, what do you want from your interactions?
- If you want an outcome to be a reduction in certain negative behaviours, express that as an outcome of the positive goal you are aiming for (such as inclusive, culturally intelligent leadership).
- What does cultural intelligence (and a successful relocation, inclusive leadership, effective team dynamics, communications with HQ, whatever the important words for your training work are) look like for you?
- What will be different?
- What will the benefits be?
- How will you know when you achieve it?

Through this process you can also highlight areas where there may be low confidence (self-efficacy) such as avoided conversations, as well as the benefits of change.

Asking questions is one of the most powerful tools you have for enabling people to create a vision if they have not arrived with one. Sometimes there is an organisational vision, but you have work to do to enable people to understand that at their individual level, within their role. I will return to the importance of questions and building your art as a questioner in Chapter 9.

Having a vision to work towards is important for CQ Drive.

3. Wellbeing

The third element that contributes to an environment conducive to developing CQ is wellbeing. There are many aspects to wellbeing. I am not going to be addressing how best to look after yourself (while hoping that you are), but instead thinking about some of the elements that contribute to a positive environment for your participants to engage and learn in.

Whether you are an internal or external trainer, the fact is that you don't always get to choose the training rooms that have the best environments in which people can have positive learning experiences. I was once at a university in London, working with the EDI (equality, diversity and inclusion) team, and they had promised me that we would be using their very best training room. It was a room that everyone in the team vied to book when delivering their own training because of the space and its quietness. These are both great assets during a training day. However, at the end of the day, most participants said how hard they had found being in a room without natural light. Despite this, they were very positive about the training. I imagine the impact could have been even better with some windows!

Various studies have found other aspects that impact on engagement, which have nothing to do with you as the trainer. These include comfort (seating, temperature, space), natural light (it has been shown not just to improve learning outcomes but also to boost mood and reduce anxiety) and noise.[8] There can, of course, be personal and cultural differences around what creates a comfortable space or one that has the right level of noise, so again don't assume your preferences are universal and ask questions around this when planning any training. The space you are in can influence how people engage and build trust, so when you can, try to work in a space that will be positive. I always try to advocate for natural light and space to move around.

---

8 There are many studies you could access about the impact of environment on different aspects from learning to generating ideas, eg Livermore 2016. See also: ucas.com/connect/blogs/how-your-surroundings-affect-way-you-study

When delivering training online to people in their work or home setting, it can also be good to encourage people, in advance, to plan to be in a spot that they feel good in, preferably one where they won't be constantly interrupted and they will be able to speak and engage.

As the trainer, you typically also have control over creating time for breaks. People need breaks. As well as ensuring there are breaks factored in, be attentive to energy levels. When they are low, giving people a short time out will typically be more productive than pushing on. When I have online groups, short, five-minute pauses seem to be appreciated as well as longer breaks, just to let people step away from the screen. Be especially mindful if there have been difficult conversations as creating space for people to step away can be helpful in enabling people to process a little and move forward.

Resistance and growth

The reasons why the participants are doing the training may have a big impact on their motivation. If someone has self-selected to do the training, they are likely to have high motivation and be ready to engage. If someone has been told they have to attend, there may be a dozen other things they would rather be doing.

People may have a deficit approach to training, meaning that they think being asked to attend any training is not so much a growth opportunity as a punishment for a lack they feel they have been perceived to have. And, as I said in Chapter 2, the training may have been commissioned due to negative events rather than a positive, such as talent development. People can find the diversity and cultural contexts they are engaging with exciting or challenging, or they could be facing discrimination or prejudice, or a combination of these.

If you work with the same type of participants, you get to build your knowledge of what kind of resistance some groups might have. Catherine often addresses resistance at the start of Master of Business Administration (MBA) programmes at Nanyang

Technological University. One complaint is that they must take the CQ component. Catherine addresses this by telling everyone that previous students get in touch to say CQ was the most valuable course they took during their MBA. They reported that when they returned to the corporate world to lead global projects, teams and negotiations, they saw the impact of culture and were prepared to deal with differences positively.

Hearing that cultural intelligence is just common sense is another type of resistance she often hears. Like many of us, what she says is that while CQ is easy to understand, it is not easy to do. Another interviewee's response to this resistance was to query, 'Whose common sense?'

Addressing resistance or concerns near the start of training doesn't magically remove them but it does acknowledge and give voice to them, and as such validates these feelings, which is important for developing trust and enabling people to feel OK in the space and make it more likely that they will hear and engage with what comes next.

CQ Drive was the capability that a few of our interviewees thought was the most important and the key one for people to think about developing, as to their minds it fuelled the others. What are your thoughts on this?

A couple of interviewees said that when they started and were working with leaders in global businesses, it felt almost embarrassingly obvious to mention motivation. With experience, they recognised that CQ Drive, especially with leaders, is not just about whether you have it or not, but also how you are leveraging that capability. How are they noticing and building it in others? Are leaders setting the tone to encourage an environment where CQ can be developed?

'*L'appétit vient en mangeant*' (the appetite comes with eating) was the quote from Justin that started this chapter. As a trainer, you want to encourage your participants, and yourself, to keep building an appetite for developing CQ Drive. As Justin said, it is often something simple such as getting people to consider who their contacts are on their phone, or social media, or who they sit next to for lunch.

This was one of the ways in which I developed my CQ Drive. I joined different business networks and became intentional about engaging with curiosity and interacting constructively when I was in dialogue with people with very different political views. My network reflects this and I'm pleased to say that when I took a CQ assessment again, I was much happier with my CQ Drive feedback. What I have found is that by expanding my view of what differences I will enjoy, grow and benefit from, or build confidence in, I have learned so much (intrinsic), it has opened up different opportunities (extrinsic) and as a result I feel more courageous (self-efficacy).

What can you share about how you have developed your CQ Drive?

Key takeaways

✧ CQ Drive is something that you feel. Are you excited by the cross-cultural engagement? Anxious? Confident?

✧ CQ Drive is not static. Events can boost or undermine it.

✧ Creating a space where there is psychological safety, consideration of the comfort and wellbeing of participants and a vision that engages people are all ingredients that contribute to effective training.

✧ Three questions that speak to the CQ Drive sub-dimensions are:

  ▲ What do you enjoy about this?

  ▲ What will the benefits be?

  ▲ What has worked well for you in the past?

✧ It is not your role as trainer to enhance someone's CQ Drive. This is their responsibility. Your role is to create a compelling vision with them and intentionally create a space where they can generate insight, then give people tips and tools so that they can make the choice to develop their CQ Drive.

Questions to consider

✧ How would you describe your CQ Drive?

✧ When is your motivation or confidence challenged during training? How have you/do you restore it?

✧ Describe a training situation when you were aware that you were engaging people to consider their CQ Drive. What were you doing? How did they respond? (Alternatively, if you have been in a training and came away feeling motivated to enhance your CQ Drive, what was the trainer or other participants doing that facilitated that?)

✧ What do you do to foster and check psychological safety during your training?

Chapter 6

Developing
CQ Knowledge

The focus is not on knowledge imparting as much as having others talking to one another, and that's the learning experience. That's how I think of it. – Samara Hakim

CQ Knowledge is about understanding how cultures shape us, how cultures are similar and different and also about knowing which aspects of any given situation are about culture. There is, of course, no end to knowledge. Despite the vastness of that statement, none of the interviewees felt that developing their CQ Knowledge was the capability they had found hardest to develop. If people have low CQ Knowledge, this is the capability that in many ways is the easiest to grow.

Acquiring knowledge is often participants' comfort zone. Typically, the people who engage in CQ development are students or workplace professionals – people who have a skill for acquiring knowledge. It can also be a comfort zone for trainers. Often people who become CQ trainers focus on knowing the content (which is, of course, super important). However, knowing and conveying that knowledge so others can understand are different things. There can be a tendency to share knowledge and want to pack too much information into sessions without taking time to consider how the information can be absorbed by participants. The 'less is more' mantra is useful here.

CQ Knowledge is so important for cultural intelligence as without it we cannot conceive of the perspective taking that is necessary for working across cultures. That said, the only CQ assessment feedback I've heard Dr David Livermore suggest may be of concern is when an individual is high in CQ Knowledge and low in all other capabilities. That may suggest that an individual could be more prone to stereotyping, relying on a bit of knowledge rather than utilising and engaging all the capabilities.

This is a pertinent thought when talking with whoever is contracting you to train. The conversations I have often start with people wanting information about the culture of specific countries or a demographic group, in terms of what they need to know to work effectively with them. Knowing is the easy bit, but on its own, CQ Knowledge will not give you the capability to relate and work effectively across cultures.

As with many fields of knowledge, when you learn a little, you suddenly see how much there is to learn. Culture is so complex, so vast and evolving, and there are just so many cultures, that we are not going to get to an end. Some people may have this in mind when doing their CQ assessments and have judged themselves low, so be mindful of this when you are discussing assessment feedback.

As trainers, what do we focus on:

- to apply our CQ Knowledge to prepare and deliver CQ training?
- to select which aspects of CQ Knowledge are most useful to share during training?

Using your CQ Knowledge to prepare

Many of the interviewees spoke about the need to apply CQ Knowledge as soon as you know you will be working with a group. In previous chapters, I have spoken about ensuring you do due diligence to discover the challenges, hopes, context, pain points and opportunities of the groups and organisation you are working for (Chapter 2), and taking the time to develop your own awareness about your cultural values and how they shape your behavioural preferences (Chapter 4).

The interviewees also spoke about how they would research the organisations they were working for online, through contacts, building knowledge both of relevant internal documents and policies and of external news stories about the organisation.

A couple of interviewees said they probably overdid this research phase on occasion, with one saying you could never overdo the research as they wanted to ensure there were no information surprises for them in the training room. There often will be surprises when working with people! There is possibly an element of how comfortable you are with uncertainty, which feeds into your decisions about how much research to do. If you think you know your CQ and can adapt to people anywhere and deliver anywhere without needing to know about the context, my encouragement would be to take some time to research the context you are going into – and then reflect on how building that into your practice enhances your planning and engagement.

Taking time to build some cultural knowledge of the groups you are working with enables you to tailor aspects of your training, which is often key to enabling people to engage positively and take away something useful. A couple of interviewees spoke about the need to avoid thinking you have a finished training product to use like a cookie cutter, with exactly the same format, examples, exercises and materials for every group.

When I'm going to be working with people in a place or sector that is unfamiliar to me, then my focus on building my knowledge ramps up. When I knew I was going to be working with bankers in Karachi, for instance, I did so much research on the bank and the country. I was aware that much of this wasn't relevant to me being able to deliver CQ training, but it achieved two things. The first was that it built my confidence. There is a link to building CQ Knowledge and building the confidence that feeds into CQ Drive. Second, through the conversations I had with people who were from Karachi or had worked there and my web searches, I was able to use some of the knowledge, which contributed to building rapport and engagement on the day.

I was aware that the body language of some people in the room changed positively at the start of the day when I was able to say 'welcome' in Urdu, and then make a response to their response to my greeting. Knowing some key phrases of the local language, if you are not using that as the key language of delivery, makes a positive impression. I just wish that once learned, I didn't then forget phrases so quickly!

Also, understand some of what is enjoyed and important within a culture. Cricket is the most popular sport in Pakistan, so I included an image of the Pakistan cricket team winning a trophy in my slides (being sure to know which trophy it was). The image generated comment, some memories and smiles, helping people to relax and share, rather than detracting from our discussion. Be sure to know what is not appropriate in the context you are in. For instance, in Pakistan, alcohol is prohibited for Muslims, so images of people socialising with a glass of wine, which are appropriate in the UK, were replaced.

It's a fairly basic CQ Knowledge task for you as a trainer to take time to notice if your audience will recognise themselves in the images you use or if the purpose of your session is evident within your images, yet I'm aware it can be overlooked. Trainers, including myself, can get used to what they use and stop noticing images or pause to think about how they could be better for the audience they are with.

CQ training is about interacting with people, but researching some differences in Pakistan's banking system was useful. Knowing that interest (*riba*) is not permitted in Islam meant that I knew products such as loans would be thought about and configured differently, with different language. Insights like this helped to build my confidence. I didn't need to be an expert, but I had enough of an insight not to assume my experiences using UK banking services would be applicable.

These small examples from one training event meant I learned (and used) new words, I planned relevant examples and used different images in my slide deck to reflect features that would resonate with the audience. For each training, use your CQ Knowledge to contextualise your approach and change aspects of your examples, questions and materials.

'A good facilitator is someone who really does their homework upfront,' was Sandra's perspective. It's important to build your knowledge of the context, and to change your input to address that context. This is also true when you are an in-house trainer. It is easy to carry assumptions about knowing the groups you are working with, or viewing them from a specific perspective from within the organisation. Take time to consider what is specific to any group you'll be working with.

Pay attention to what is going on in the world. What are the news events that will be uppermost in people's minds in the places you are going to deliver training? Many of the interviewees spoke about the importance of keeping informed for several reasons, ranging from drawing examples or insights from current events that help to develop understanding (which is a different thing to sharing your views or position) to being aware of the impact events may be having on your participants. Whatever the niche or purpose of your training, whether leadership, relocation, inclusion, marketing or business mergers, keep adding to your knowledge.

For example, Fenny researches and is always looking at how differences in aspects of life such as technology have changed how young leaders go about communicating and getting things done. She plans how to weave that knowledge into her CQ training to get people focused on how to relate better across generations. What is your interest or niche? Keep deepening your knowledge.

Along with deepening knowledge, some interviewees spoke to the need to keep broadening your knowledge. Anindita spoke to this. If you speak about CQ within its own distinct box, you can miss that it is in the combination of many things, be that anthropology, psychology, business, current affairs, history or sociology. Her advice to trainers just starting out is not to be too narrow in thinking about cultural intelligence, but to read and view widely.

What aspects of CQ Knowledge are most useful to share during training?

Do I hear you thinking 'Enough already!'? There really is no end to knowledge, so what are the considerations for deciding what to include? Key to providing training in CQ Knowledge is enabling people to grasp key concepts about cultural knowledge in a way that is accessible so that they can 'see' where and how culture is showing up in themselves and others, and then create space for people to acknowledge and layer on the complexity.

There are four sub-dimensions to the CQ Knowledge capability. If you are using CQ assessments, you may want to briefly talk about each so that people can reflect on each point in their personal CQ feedback reports.

1. Cultural systems

Systems grow out of culture. The laws, economic policies and educational systems both at a national and organisational level. Culture impacts how, and what, policies and systems are put in place.

Which systems are key to the success of the people and purpose of your training?

2. Values and norms

Which values drive the implementation of those systems? What do day-to-day interactions consist of? Which beliefs are core to the organisation or person? There is a vast body of work showing how culture shapes our values, and vice versa.

As discussed in Chapter 4, all the interviewees spoke of introducing and discussing cultural values, many near the start of sessions.

People often have 'aha' moments of revelation when talking about cultural values as they reflect on how they have shown up in their experiences – seeing new ways to interpret events or understand what drives them.

It's a discussion that creates understanding around the reality that we all come into experiences and relationships with different values and behavioural preferences.

Key to your preparation is preparing examples that enable participants to 'see' how the values you are introducing show up in their context and in relation to the key theme and purpose of the training.

3. Sociolinguistics

When we bring knowledge of language and social groups together, we have sociolinguistics. This is not just about knowing other languages (although that is, of course, a great gateway to learning about and interacting with people from a different culture) – it is also about noticing the rules of language within a specific context.

For example, I've heard many professionals in the UK (in all sorts of organisations, ranging from businesses to universities to hospitals) bemoan the lack of courtesy they are shown by colleagues (or students, or customers) from overseas because of a request that did not include the word 'please'. There is often energy being used in feeling the slight, rather than the energy being used to notice other ways the person is showing respect or understanding how polite requests are made in the first language of the person that may not translate into English, or using their energy to engage positively and help someone understand the impact the absence of the word 'please' has on them and may have on others in the UK.

One of the examples I frequently hear people talk about in relation to sociolinguistic knowledge is whether people are direct or indirect. If you were at work and heard the phrase 'the window is open', would you understand that as an observational statement or an instruction to close it? It could be either. Context and meaning are often interrelated.

If you are in a new culture, or in a culturally diverse setting, even if people are speaking the same language, there is a high chance that the same words will be understood differently.

- What observations and questions do your participants have about language in the context they are in?
- What can you do to enable people to see how culture creates different meanings and possibilities? (In the next chapter, words and meaning are explored with some exercise suggestions.)

4. Leadership

Leadership is about aligning and enabling others to achieve goals in any setting, whether in the classroom or the boardroom. The question is not what is good or bad leadership, but what will enable us to be effective leaders in this context?

Cultural intelligence is a stronger predictor of leadership success in multicultural settings than IQ, EQ (emotional intelligence) and lived experience (Livermore 2024). A good resource for thinking about this is the Globe leadership survey, a large-scale study of cultural practices, leadership ideals and generalised and interpersonal trust in 150 countries, in collaboration with nearly 500 researchers (globeproject.com). While most contributors in various industries and countries identified similar characteristics as positive for leadership, the behaviours people would need to see as evidence a leader had that trait varied. For example, people everywhere want leaders who are trustworthy.

Over the past few years, I've been connected with some business leaders in South Africa who were talking about how they couldn't really trust an American organisation they worked with as it often seemed that people just disappeared and they didn't get information as to why. Building relationships was key to them, so having people in key functions be replaced without a story about why felt unsettling, whereas the other perspective would be that a person is free to move on (or a company is free to move them on), with all related information being considered private to the individual. The important aspect is that the function is being continued with the new person recruited into the role.

Which information is considered private and which information is considered necessary for the relationship can vary substantially around the world (and be written into the laws – cultural systems – of the place). When you are in one system, it is easy to overlook how things are impacting those with whom you have relationships who are operating in different systems.

Leading across different systems would not be about disclosing information deemed personal in one context, but it could be about acknowledging the relationship and as a minimum having time for a conversation, which can help with building understanding; while without a conversation, it is left to assumptions, judgement from one perspective and corroding of trust (which may well be hidden to one party).

This can also be a rich discussion to have when looking at organisational values along with cultural values. How are the organisation's values being manifested in behaviours? The more diverse the organisation, then potentially there are many ways to demonstrate these values, which can start an eye-opening conversation if leaders think through what that may mean for their leadership or for inclusion or innovation.

What aspects of your experience, or the context of the participants, will enable you to speak to these different elements of CQ Knowledge?

I've contracted with different parts of the same university. Their policies cover the whole university (cultural systems), but my experience from the outside is that they are implemented differently. For example, how decision making is devolved (values and norms plus leadership) can be quite different in different parts of the same university, even for very similar work engagements. This indicates to me that my language may need to shift depending on how the authority for decision making is being configured (sociolinguistics and leadership).

When facilitating, I often hear people present both sides of a value (the norms around how direct communication is, for example) and say things such as, 'You can just ask people to be direct, if that is how you want to receive information.'

In his book *Beyond Culture* (1981), Edward Hall writes: 'Culture hides much more than it reveals, and, strangely, it hides itself most effectively from its own participants.' Therefore it can be the case that if you ask someone to be more direct, they may not understand what your issue is because to their mind their message is obvious! In the contexts in which they have been operating, their communications were understood.

This was brought home to me when my triplet sons were small. I have always considered myself to be a clear, explicit, direct speaker. I used to ask them to do small tasks, saying things such as, 'Would you like to take this through to the kitchen?' They would look at me and say 'No', typically in unison.

'What do you mean, no?' I'd ask. 'I've asked you to take this through to the kitchen!' They would look at me with confusion and say, 'No, you didn't.' This conversation took place several times before it dawned on me that the phrase 'would you like to' is not a direct, clear instruction to do something. I was 36 when my sons were born. I had worked with colleagues and students from around the world. That's quite a long time to live without realising that my communication style wasn't nearly as direct as I had assumed it to be. And while I still ask them 'Would you like to...', there is now a shared understanding that this is an order!

As a trainer, have a think about occasions when aspects of your approach to doing things has been hidden from you. This is easier done in conversation with another person who knows how you communicate and go about getting things done. If you are able to share some stories, it can help to deepen conversations and learning. What does the way things are done in your context tell you about yourself that you had perhaps not been cognisant of?

David said the key thing he wanted people to take away from thinking about CQ Knowledge was that they see themselves as a product of the cultures in which they operate. This is important as we take ourselves into every context.

One of the elements I like to stress about CQ is that when you are working with other people, you are always in the position of not knowing much. The quote about how our culture is often hidden to us is also true. Accepting that we can't know everything that contributes to a person and culture is part of what enables us to draw on the other CQ capabilities.

We are living in the age of information. In many societies, information is at our fingertips and a quick search away on our devices. A conversation about critical thinking, how we assess which information has validity, considering when we are responding to anecdote and when to good research, is also worth exploring. When in discussion with individuals, what they share about their experience is always valid. It is not a reason to assume their experience is the same for everyone you think is in their group.

If you are working with an organisation that deals specifically with certain groups, include generalisations about the cultural values or norms of those groups. However, focus as much on 'culture' that you have here as looking at the culture 'over there'. Which behaviours or systems create the rub for the people you are with? What could people be misinterpreting? How could they build more trust? CQ Knowledge is about building your understanding of how culture has shaped and impacted you (and the groups you are part of), which impacts on how we interact and perceive others.

Part of what a good trainer brings to these discussions is reminding everyone about human complexity. We are all multi-dimensional. We all have lots of layers. Before opening or concluding a discussion on cultural values, you can broaden it out by sharing a slide or material about many elements of our identities, such as race, ethnicity, parenting status, body shape, neurodiversity, accent, among many others, to emphasise how these aspects overlay cultural values and behavioural preferences.

To Anindita's point about broadening your knowledge, she had said that if she focuses only on the cultural values, she may miss a lot of other dimensions that are working along with them in the scenarios that participants share. 'It could be generation plus cultural values, or it could be gender plus cultural values, or it could be caste plus cultural values. And if I'm too focused on only cultural values, I might not see the other cultural dimensions.'

In Jennifer's work developing inclusive leaders within the UK's public services, the broad thinking about difference sits at the heart of her work, with culture being one aspect of the differences we have. Vital to this is that CQ Knowledge creates lightbulb moments for people to see that it is often the invisible aspects of cultural difference that are creating barriers to inclusion. As Sandra said, it is not always an easy conversation, but the dynamic of how cultures interact and view different aspects of identity can be rich and insightful.

This brings me to Samara's quote at the start of this chapter and her perspective that, as a trainer, the importance lies not so much on imparting information as creating space and opportunity for people to speak, share insights and develop together. At the end of the day, if knowledge was all that was required, people have access to the internet. Our value as trainers is being able to deepen, broaden and engage our participants in thinking through how these cultural differences are showing up and impacting in their context and what that may mean for their ambitions.

In Justin's words, 'The one thing that I've learned is that CQ training is only effective when you engage people. Their experiences will be the spice of their whole training. All you do is provide the framework; their stories become, and then confirm, the knowledge.'

The longer I have been a trainer in this field, the more I have come to appreciate the maxim 'less is more' when it comes to thinking about what to include when discussing CQ Knowledge.

Tom shared that in the early days of his work, many of his contracts were related to outsourcing services from Australia to the Philippines, Malaysia or India, so much of his work was focused on knowledge transfer – how to communicate with the people of the country the process was being outsourced to and vice versa; how do they understand the mindset and communication style of the Australians?

As CQ trainers, we know that knowledge is important, but only one of four equally important capabilities. As Tom says, know your own value add. Our role is to curate some key bits of knowledge to enable people to think about and 'see' culture and then to create the invitation for them to explore how they are seeing the impact within their context, or within the challenges or opportunities they are addressing.

All the interviewees spoke about cultural values, and it makes so much sense to include a discussion of some of them as they show up in all other aspects, be that cultural systems, sociolinguistics or leadership, whatever the purpose of your training – whether it's about improving team productivity, international business outcomes or local inclusion. It's key for building self-awareness of what your preferences and potential biases may be. However, if you are using the CQ assessments from the CQ Center, there are ten behavioural preferences listed and quite a few of the interviewees would just select three to seven for discussion to enable people to go deeper. (This very much depends on time, number of sessions and purpose.)

If you have configured your training programme to talk about cultural values before opening up thinking on the four capabilities, when you cover CQ Knowledge you can select so many things that can resonate with your purpose. Your role will be to limit how many as people can only absorb so much, which means part of what you want to do is whet appetites to encourage continuous curiosity to learn.

Models of trust, communication styles,[9] bias, micro-aggressions, reviewing where culture is showing up in aspects of policy implementation, processes, or staff or client feedback, are all elements that could help you highlight cultural knowledge that is relevant to your training.

---

9 On communication styles, I may draw on the work of Watson et al (1995). This considers that how we listen and communicate may reflect the emphasis we place on one of four factors: action, content, people, time – all of which can be influenced by culture and all of which may be hidden to us without attention.

For example, when I've been told that trust is an issue, I like to take time to consider models of trust, such as one David Livermore cites in *Driven by Difference* (2016). He shares that there are five factors that consistently emerge when calculating trust in a work context, and each of these are impacted by culture. They are likeability, competency, intentions, reliability and reputation. All the factors are relevant, and of course the context and reason you are thinking about trust matter, but most of us have one or two of these factors that are dominant.

I can reflect that when I was young, it was drilled into me that if I'd said I was going to be somewhere or do something, then I had to do that, regardless of what better opportunity or reason to not do that thing emerged. I'm aware that my sons have had the same drilled into them. I can see a pattern in my life of why reliability would be the key factor for me.

When I ask people to go to a place in the room that represents one of the five factors that is most important to them (or select on a poll if virtual), it has often resulted in a discussion in which participants are incredulous about other people's thinking. It opens up an avenue for understanding how culture has impacted them in ways that influence when and how we feel trust. While trust is a universal human instinct, culture and experiences shape what makes us offer or feel trust. Realising this opens up an opportunity for reflecting on and thinking through how people can go about building trust.

There are many models of trust and this speaks to the suggestion earlier in this chapter about consistently deepening your knowledge about the themes you engage with during your CQ training. Think less about how you impart knowledge and more about how to create opportunities to open up insights.

The limits to CQ Knowledge

At the beginning of this chapter, I wrote that CQ Knowledge is about thinking through which aspects of a situation are about culture and which aren't, as not everything is. One example is that poverty is not culture. When working with certain professionals such as people who work with refugees, I find it useful to have a conversation about how there are many factors influencing how we act or react. Whether our basic human needs for food, shelter and security are being met is one of those things. It's important not to consider all behaviours as cultural as some are reactions to a situation. There is always complexity.

There is no end to knowledge and there are always knowledge gaps. For example, if you are using the CQ assessments, you may see that they refer to ten cultural clusters within the behavioural preference profile (see Livermore 2013). There are currently more than eight billion people in the world and just over 9 per cent of them are in Europe, yet four of the ten clusters are wholly European and another includes European countries (UK and Ireland being in the cluster named Anglo). I suspect that this is not because Europe is so rich in terms of cultural differences compared to the rest of the world, but that it reflects where most of the research has been done.

When I was with the British Council, I worked with a project team that was located across nine Arab countries. Arab is one cluster of the ten global clusters. I think of the Gulf States, the North African Arab countries and the countries around the eastern Mediterranean as culturally distinct. Yes, there are commonalities, as there are across Europe if you use enough of a wide-angled lens. I am unfamiliar with sub-Saharan Africa, but it is vast and I suspect that more research (especially research initiated from within these regions) would result in there being far more cultural clusters, or perhaps fewer in Europe when looked at from an outsider's eye.

Sometimes when I've worked with American students in the UK and I've been told they have left the US for the first time, I do an exercise where I introduce Hofstede's onion model of culture (Hofstede 1991). This model has values at the core (which in Hofstede's view do not change much) and then layers that comprise rituals, heroes and symbols of a culture.

When I put people into small groups and ask them to populate some of the aspects they would put into the three categories of rituals, heroes and symbols of culture, with some groups thinking about the US and some thinking about the UK, one of the things I notice in the group discussions is that those thinking about their own American culture have disagreements or don't reach easy conclusions. For example, a conversation I've heard is about whether the president is a symbol or a hero, whereas the groups thinking about the UK typically have no problem deciding that the British royal family is a UK cultural hero. What often comes across during a debrief is describing a culture that you haven't experienced feels easier, but it's a stereotype rather than nuanced.

To date, research on CQ has focused on cross-cultural differences in the way people think, feel and act due to their experience of cultures they have been socialised in. The research demonstrates that building our CQ reduces our anxiety and enhances our capability to work and relate well when we interact and work with people who have been socialised to think, feel and act differently in their cultures.

However, Soon Ang writes that in the future she intends to also focus on CQ through a lens based on social injustice and disparities in status and power: 'Attributes such as nationality, ethnicity and gender evoke inequality and power imbalance due to sociohistorical events such as colonisation, oppression, and marginalisation.' These differences in status (which are referred to as vertical differentiation, whereas the cultural values we recognise are based on horizontal differentiation) create different concerns for people from the dominant (or majority) groups versus the non-dominant (or minority) groups (Ang et al 2021).

As practitioners, knowing that the research is always evolving is important and an aspect of what we can share with others when useful. We are always learning and there is no end to knowledge.

Key takeaways

✧ The opportunity to train any group of people is an opportunity to use your CQ. Use your CQ Knowledge to build your knowledge of the context, challenges and opportunities of each group you work with.

✧ Use this knowledge to adapt your content, what you emphasise, your materials and your examples.

✧ There is no end to CQ Knowledge. Keep expanding yours through books, networks, films, podcasts, travel, news sites, learning new languages and conversations. The possibilities are endless to go deep and/or to go broad.

✧ A key aspect of CQ Knowledge is that, when working with others, there is always more you don't know than you do.

✧ You have taken years to build your CQ Knowledge. Your participants will be in different places. You can't convey all of your knowledge during one training programme. Curate what you focus on and do so with the purpose of the training in mind (and have good reference materials for people to refer to afterwards).

✧ Facilitate discovery. This embeds knowledge.

Questions to consider

✧ What are the three key pieces of CQ Knowledge that have been most influential for you when you consider the key purpose of your training? (Team effectiveness, inclusion, leadership – there may be different answers when you think of different groups you train.)

✧ How often do you change the training materials you use with your audiences in mind?

✧ What impact would selecting only three aspects of CQ Knowledge have on you? Does it seem too little? Does it help you decide what to include in your training?

✧ How do you and your participants source knowledge and decide what is reliable or useful in the situation?

✧ What are your thoughts on Samara's view that learning is not fostered by imparting knowledge, but by having participants discuss and share their perspectives?

⤊ Do you think this would apply in your training contexts?

⤊ What are the factors that make you think so?

Chapter 7

Developing CQ Strategy

CQ Strategy is where you develop the muscle to use your knowledge in a proactive, practical, day-to-day way.
– Buhle Dlamini

How often have you received some information and jumped straight into action? A key capability of cultural intelligence is taking a pause to plan, build awareness, pay attention, check and reflect in order to use your cultural knowledge in ways that are considered and appropriate to the people and context you are in and to achieve your intended purpose.

Known as metacognition, or thinking about thinking, CQ Strategy is about developing the habit of noticing, thinking about and planning how to respond to the impacts of culture. Buhle described it as the difference between being proactive and being reactive, which I liked as a descriptor as who doesn't want to be proactive?

You may also hear people say that being quick is their strength. Research says that if you are a leader in a complex, diverse organisation who makes good decisions without having high cultural intelligence, you'll make even better, more effective ones if you enhance your (and your organisation's) CQ (Rockstuhl & Van Dyne 2018).

As with CQ Drive, three of the interviewees said this was the capability that they had found hardest to develop. Comments they shared included:

- 'Lucy, I'm an entrepreneur. I get an idea or opportunity and want to pursue it immediately.'
- 'The context around me is very short-term orientated, which doesn't encourage me to pause, plan and reflect.'

When I asked them if they had experience of better outcomes when they took time to think about who they were going to be interacting with and developing flexible plans, the answer was emphatically yes.

Five interviewees said that for them this was the capability they tried to emphasise most in their training. David said that while many intercultural people talk about awareness and sense making, fewer mention these as key in the way that CQ Strategy does.

While cultural intelligence is not difficult to understand as a concept, it is not easy to do! What makes it hard is building that habit of not just being reactive to events and data, but taking time to be aware of how culture might play out in any situation and plan for that. When we are stressed, or time poor, or working in a complex situation (or all three), our instinct is often to go with quick reactions. Catherine tells her students, 'I can tell you about the cultural differences and the dimensions, but the day you will need that knowledge, most of you won't think about it. Most of you won't remember it. This has to do with how your brain is wired.'

Daniel Kahneman's work on the psychology of judgement and decision making found that we operate with two thinking systems. System 1 is a fast-thinking mode that relies on intuition and past experiences. In contrast, System 2 is a slow-thinking mode, where we engage in deliberate, logical analysis. This requires more effort. In his book, *Thinking, Fast and Slow* (2013), Kahneman writes, 'A general "law of least effort" applies to cognitive as well as physical exertion. The law asserts that if there are several ways of achieving the same goal, people will eventually gravitate to the least demanding course of action. In the economy of action, effort is a cost, and the acquisition of skill is driven by the balance of benefits and costs. Laziness is built deep into our nature.'

You can understand why we jump from a bit of information to action, and why assumption and bias so often weave their way into our decisions and actions. Giving us hope, what Kahneman's work also found is that when we become more skilled at something, the effort required becomes less. All of the contributors to this book can attest to that.

The habit of seeing, paying attention to and planning for cultural differences is the muscle that Buhle speaks to in his quote that starts this chapter. To use that 'muscle' when you need it, you need to practise using it when you are relaxed and not in a high-stakes context. However, if you find yourself in a complex scenario or difficult conversation you hadn't expected or planned for, one small practical tip that has really helped me to stop myself just reacting is the practice of taking a long, slow, deep breath that pushes out the belly.

If there are behaviours I don't understand, or a question that throws me, or there is continued discord between participants, I have found that there is no better way to calm myself and create the space for me to have a think about ways in which I could respond to the situation than to take a deep breath. It is an action that enables you to go from reacting to being able to take stock and be proactive (BBC 2021). A deep breath with participants is an exercise I sometimes weave into my training sessions, especially when the topic includes themes such as difficult conversations. (With thanks to Pete Quinn, who made this a regular feature when we worked together on conscious decision-making programmes with an NHS Trust.)

However, to be able to draw on it as a technique, it requires you to have practised it yourself. In conversations with family and friends, take a moment to draw a deep breath and observe what impact it has on you and whether anyone else seems to notice. That slow, deep breath is a useful response when you are wondering about what may be going on in a situation and how you can respond to it in that moment.

So, how do you and your participants build the CQ muscle so that you notice culture and crucially develop ways to respond to what is going on and plan effectively? The interviewees talked about the importance of getting people to root their thinking about CQ Strategy within their context and challenges.

Awareness

The knowledge of how culture has shaped us and creates values and behavioural preferences contributes to awareness. Keep building your CQ Knowledge regarding how cultures are similar and different as it is necessary for building CQ Strategy. Research by Dr Tasha Eurich found that, while 95 per cent of people think they are self-aware, only 10–15 per cent of people actually are, and because leaders often find it hard to get honest feedback, they tend to be less self-aware than others (Eurich 2017). A key aspect of training for the interviewees was creating exercises for developing awareness in participants as to how we look out and make sense of the world and how we may be perceived.

Suggested exercises
Noticing assumptions

Create an exercise that draws attention to what your participants are first aware of when they receive information about people (whether visual, textual or auditory information).

The interviewees ask people to respond to visuals or a text, then ask them something along the lines of 'Write whatever comes into your head first', having let people know if they will be sharing their responses or not. Then they facilitate a discussion on the meaning of the words 'observation' and 'assumption'. Participants are asked to sort their responses into 'observations' and 'assumptions' and a third group, 'other', as people may have had a question come into their head or made an association such as, 'That reminds me of my mother.'

If people look at an image and write down how many people were in the picture, the colour of something or a detail such as a person smiling – that is an observation. If they write that people are arguing, that they're neighbours or colleagues, or that they're listening, it creates space to ask, 'How do you know?' The rule of an exercise like this is that you can only call it an observation if you can definitely say it is fact. To figure out what is going on in a picture, or how people feel, you would need to ask clarifying questions. There's an image I often share that leads to conversations where people say, 'But they are clearly having an argument. It is an observation', only for someone else to say, 'I thought it was a couple about to kiss.' The images I use are not designed to be controversial or intentionally puzzling; they're just people interacting in some way. It often amazes me what people see and project onto them.

When you ask people if they have mainly listed observations or assumptions, in most groups most people will be sharing assumptions. The interviewees shared my experience of this. Assumptions are what come into most of our heads when we look out at the world. It is not about stopping these assumptions; it is about taking the time to notice and check them, rather than react and plan on the basis of our assumptions. When I'm working with American students, usually at least one will quip, 'To assume is to make an ass out of you and me!' Ass-u-me! Sometimes – but mostly, assuming is just being human, and assumptions can be negative, neutral or positive. When I go into a training room, I carry the assumption that people are going to engage (and I have plans for what I can change if that isn't the case). Our assumptions can contribute to our confidence and enable us to do what we do. The problem is not that we have assumptions, but that frequently we do not take the time to recognise and listen to the assumptions that are in our heads. Without paying attention to our assumptions, our actions can then flow from incorrect or unhelpful assumptions.

This was highlighted for me following a pilot leadership development programme that I was managing for the British Council, which had participants from Jordan, Egypt and the UK for its first year before widening out across nine Arab countries. During an event with participants from the three countries in Amman, Jordan, people worked in circles of chairs of about ten people in small groups, with the facilitators talking to the whole room of about 150 people (using simultaneous translators) to brief and debrief activities. Every so often over the course of the three days, small groups of Egyptians and/or Jordanians would break into song and/or dance.

I've never delivered a training to professionals in the UK where participants have spontaneously started to sing or dance! During evaluation interviews a few months following the programme, a participant from the UK who was in the police force said that the dancing and singing had made him question his assumptions. In the past he had viewed this behaviour, in contexts where he couldn't see the reason why people may be singing and dancing, as whipping themselves up and getting ready for trouble, and would plan on that basis. This enabled us to reflect that in the UK, people are generally not very comfortable with expressing their emotion, whether grief or joy, outside specific events.

Paying attention to what is going on in people's heads is a crucial part of planning. How people engage, intervene or decide who to speak to before reaching a decision impacts outcomes. Take time to pay attention to what is going on in your head and determine if that is shared with the people with whom you work. Shared assumptions may sound positive, but they can create gaps in awareness that can stop people finding solutions to challenges.

A head of teaching and learning in a university science field once said to me that an exercise like this made them see that the biggest assumption they had made was that they only dealt with facts. This assumption had been drilled into her thinking as a scientist and she realised that she was therefore unaware of the many assumptions that had been made.

Sometimes you do need to follow assumptions. It's the best you have to go on, but it is useful to be clear that it is an assumption you are exploring, or that you are basing plans on, as that creates the possibility of pivoting and changing to a better direction or plan if and when more information comes to you.

In most groups, most people look out at the world and instantly start interpreting, while paying little attention to the fact that this is what they are doing. However, there are people who just make observations, who process the world in a literal fashion, and for whom the norms of others who jump to assumptions can be disorientating and confusing.

I find it is worthwhile to take time to discuss neurodiversity and how neurodivergent and neurotypical people can often process the world very differently. For people in the room who do process the world in a literal fashion, this exercise can be an eye opener as it demonstrates not that others are able to 'see' different facts, but that they are often making up the 'facts'. The worth of people who are literal in their processing of stimuli around them is clear in these discussions.

Groups and individuals

I want you to imagine that you are training a group of 20 people in a room on the first floor of an office building. You are going to take everyone down the escalators, out of the building and across the road at the pedestrian crossing in front of the building, and into the coffee shop opposite. Can you imagine the 20 people going down the escalator and across the road into the shop? Chances are you can imagine a group of people doing this.

Now try to imagine each of the 20 people individually as they do this. Who has taken a bag with them? How are they carrying it? What is each person wearing? Who is chatting? In smaller groups of what number? Who is silent? What are they thinking about? Who finds walking hard? How are they adjusting? Even for quite a small group of 20, it is too much of a cognitive load to think of each person individually within the group behaving in their distinct ways. (This idea is adapted from a larger discussion in *Gendered Species* by Tamas David-Barrett, published in 2024.) When thinking of people in groups, we create a group identity.

With our propensity to think in groups and be lazy in our thinking, it calls on us to be mindful of the groupings that we make.

We may also have a strong cultural preference whether we identify with the group or as an individual. When I was coaching a senior executive who had moved from China to take up a senior management role with a European multinational business, one aspect of leading his teams in Europe that surprised him was the tendency for team members to assert individual requirements. For example, he shared how one of the teams was going to have to spend a week working at a location a couple of hours' travel away from their usual office. He said there were various options. People could travel each day or they could stay in a hotel for the week close to the location. To his surprise, everyone wanted something different. Some wanted the hotel only on certain nights and those nights were different for each colleague.

He said that, in his experience in China, that would not have happened. If he had laid out the scenario, there would have been silence before one person spoke to say whether they would travel daily or stay in the hotel and then everyone would have agreed and the group would have done the same thing.

Whether we identify more with the group or with individual interests is cultural, but our propensity to think of people in groups is human. Stereotyping happens when we think in groups. The beauty of stereotypes is that they let us sum up and describe group characteristics. The downside is that, at best, this is always a sweeping generalisation.

Which groups are your participants talking about? Group stereotypes are useful for sharing ideas and planning (whether you are thinking about emailing instructions to students or designing a marketing campaign for a new product). In addition to the planning, think through how you will reach or respond to the individuals who do not share the expected group characteristics, whatever the information about expected group characteristics was based on. We often get one piece of data or an anecdote and attribute it to the group without taking the time to consider how representative it is.

As a trainer, you need to consider when to notice the individual and when it is useful to draw on the power of the group. In a training scenario, you may be responding to an individual's question, but the responses and your actions are heard and observed by everyone in the group. You are always communicating with the whole group. You can sometimes focus on one individual who is being positive or negative and forget to relate that to the group. Training, as with many things, is a dance between engaging at the individual level and the group level. And you can create positive learning environments by pulling on the power of the group. One of the reasons for taking time to agree behaviours at the beginning of the session is that it helps to create that group power, when you can remind individuals of group agreements. This typically helps individuals to feel secure within the group.

As a trainer, you will benefit from asking the same questions that you might ask your participants to make in their roles:

- What do you want for the group?
- What are the goals for the group?

Answering these questions and being clear so that everyone understands what the goals are and how they can get behind a goal contributes to CQ Drive. CQ Strategy requires you to think about how different approaches can contribute differently to achieve those goals and what that requires from you as a trainer (or leaders, students or whatever) to make this possible.

- What are the different ways in which individuals can contribute, depending on their norms and preferences?
- What different ways are there for people to give feedback?
- How many ways can you think of that will convey the same message?
- How will you test which messages have most impact here?

In advance and during any training, hold that each person with you is unique, therefore you don't know what to expect from anyone, while also trying to create a group that gels and can learn together.

Limits of language

I want you to imagine that I have dropped my jacket on the floor. Do you have a word for the shape a dropped jacket would create?

If you have thought of a shape word, or perhaps something like 'it is in a heap', are you confident that if you asked a group of people to draw the shape word or 'in a heap' that everyone would be able to draw something that looked like my dropped jacket? Our languages have limitations. I frequently have the radio on in the background, without fully listening. I'm aware I heard something like the above. I know it was on BBC Radio 4, but I've no idea what the programme was or who was speaking.

Along with there being many gaps in what we have words for, we also have different perceptions of what words mean. This was highlighted to me years ago when I was talking to a student who had come from Mumbai in India to study in Scotland at the University of Strathclyde in the centre of Glasgow. He asked me where all the people were and where people went to work. I thought it was obvious that people were coming into Glasgow city centre to work and confess I couldn't understand his confusion, until I went on my first trip to Mumbai. I was brought up in a small, rural town in north-east Scotland; for me Glasgow was the big, bustling city. It could fit into Mumbai many, many times over. Experiencing Mumbai instantly made me realise that words such as 'busy' or 'noisy' come with totally different frames of reference.

Add to this that you may often be working in groups where there are different first languages and you have to hold that there are many different understandings taking place in the training room and in the lives of your participants. As Justin shared, the language you are speaking is not aways the language you mean.

Words such as effective, inclusive, diligent, belonging, charismatic, time wasting, allyship, trustworthy, success, all of which you may use or hear during CQ training, can be even harder to pin down. What do the key words that are used in your training mean to you? Can you be flexible and hear that they may mean something different to the people you are training? How flexible?

People can become very attached to their words and definitions, and I've been in spaces where participants want to argue about exact definitions. It can be useful to have questions and strategies for showing (rather than telling) that while language is shared, meaning can be personal.

As with the dance between group and individual, as a trainer you also need to be able hold the tension between making meaning in a group while not getting too bogged down in definitions.

Your invisible knapsack

- What aspects of your identity have brought you unearned advantage or disadvantage?
- How does that impact on how you look out, notice, experience and interpret what is going on around you?

For some interviewees, this was an important discussion that they brought into their training as part of developing the CQ Strategy awareness capability. A metaphor for privilege is that it is an invisible, weightless rucksack that has special provisions in it that were not earned and are frequently unacknowledged. In an interview with *The New Yorker* (Rothman 2014), Peggy McIntosh spoke about how her work considering disparities around gender led to her also noticing the systems that create disparities in race within her American context.

McIntosh said that she asked herself, on a daily basis, 'What do I have that I didn't earn?' These reflections led to her realisation that she was embedded in the systems that oppressed others and had never been encouraged to acknowledge and notice them. In 1988, McIntosh wrote a paper called 'White privilege and male privilege', which influenced how many understood, shared and contributed to discussions about how different aspects of our identities may bring us the privilege of unearned advantage. McIntosh wrote that our privilege can change from day to day, minute to minute, depending on the context around us.

As a trainer, what is interesting is learning how this reflective and autobiographical approach transformed how McIntosh approached her work as an educator. She minimised lectures and replaced them with students sharing experiences by answering questions. Responses were uninterrupted, given a set time and done by all. Inviting people to share experiences encourages listening, whereas inviting opinion can lead to argument. Through listening to the experiences of others, patterns can emerge and reveal that while we are all unique as individuals, we are also all part of systems.

In the notes for facilitators in McIntosh's essay cited above, the suggestion is to invite people to come up with their own autobiographical lists of privilege, thinking broadly about their life and experience. Whether or not this is a conversation you would bring into your training sessions, I would recommend that you take the time to do it for yourself. A few brief thoughts from my experience of advantage/privilege are:

- I was loved and cared for by my parents. It has given me the privilege of security in my worth.
- When I started school aged five, I loved it. A year later, my younger brother started at the same school. In a short time, he had developed a stutter. A difference? I am white. My brother, being half Pakistani, has brown skin and that difference had a profound impact on the daily interactions we experienced. I don't think my white skin has drawn any comment, let alone insult, during my life in Scotland.
- I have triplet sons, which meant I had a large pram! Navigating my city with that pram made me acutely aware of how much of our built environment, from entering shops to accessing local train stations, has been designed only with people who are able to walk independently in mind. Add to that behaviours such as parking on pavements and I realised how easy it had been for me to move around where I wanted to and access facilities.

This is a snippet from a much longer list. The process of thinking through the question of the advantages and disadvantages my identity and experience have brought me has had various outcomes:

* It has enabled me to feel gratitude about aspects of my life I had paid no attention to.
* It has enabled me to notice more about systems I am part of.
* It has expanded my capacity to listen with empathy (which in turn has reduced defensive reactions to information shared by others).

For some years I was a volunteer facilitator with the organisation Soliya (soliya.net), whose aim is to promote constructive dialogue with students around the world. At the time I was volunteering, it was for students in Arab countries and the US. Now it works globally. It is a truly fabulous programme working across a semester to enable young adults to approach differences constructively and with empathy. Questions are always the key tool of any trainer, and as a Soliya facilitator, an important aspect was to use questions to enable speakers to think through the opinions they were sharing.

* When did you come to that opinion?
* Who, and/or which events, influenced your thinking on this?
* What did the people around you believe?

Questions that root people in their experience enable everyone to see that we are all shaped by different experiences. It encourages empathy and tends to be constructive. It was great when, halfway through the semester, the students would start to ask each other these types of questions rather than argue their point. People would become more open to holding nuance and being open to change through the process of sharing their experience and listening to the experience of others.

UNESCO has accessible tools, methodologies and case studies about using story circles as an approach for fostering respectful, peaceful and inclusive cultures. Their methodology for sharing stories engages all three modes of learning: cognitive, socio-emotional and behavioural, which can mean emotional connections are made with other participants (Deardorff 2020).

As a trainer, you may not be working with people over an extended period of time, and change takes time. What you can always do is ensure that people's experience and feelings are heard and acknowledged. As humans, we can want to demonstrate that we relate to the experiences of others and say things like 'I know how you feel' or 'Everyone shares this experience'. For example, during a session, someone shared that they had recently moved home and had been anxious about how the neighbours might respond to them being in a same-sex couple. Another participant shared that when she moved house, she had been worried about how the neighbours would respond, saying it was human nature to worry about the reactions of new neighbours. I asked if one of her concerns was how the neighbours would react to her sexuality. Her negative response led to her recognising that this was a concern she did not carry and had not thought about for others. We all have different experiences of similar events. It can feel like not being heard when someone shares an experience and it is reduced to a variation on what everyone goes through. Learn and encourage your participants to listen and absorb what they are hearing. Model this and encourage it throughout any sessions. And think about your questions. Do you really want to know what someone thinks about something, or would it be more useful to ask about their experiences?

I've witnessed Jennifer lead powerful discussions on the theme of privilege within her training sessions. She starts with her own autobiographical list of advantage and disadvantage, which draws from many areas of her life. Then she asks participants a series of questions that they do not have to share responses to but which highlight experience. Then she asks if anyone wishes to share their experience of doing the exercise.

What was your experience of doing this exercise?

This is a question that often opens up great insights and discussions during CQ training sessions and enables participants to recognise how they look out at the world.

Questions

Each of the suggestions for raising awareness involves questions. This is key for participants to take away. Without being open and curious, it is nigh on impossible to raise awareness of how being shaped by the cultures we are part of are influencing us, let alone others.

It is also important for you as a trainer.

- What do you know?
- What do you not know?
- What could be impacting this interaction that you cannot see?
- Who else do I need to speak to or get information from?

I will consider the art of questions more fully in the next chapter, but for now think about the assumptions that you or your participants have made about the people they engage with, or their purpose, and enable them to think through questions that would give them a fuller picture.

Planning

Taking the time to build our awareness, recognise our assumptions and bias, and consider what elements are creating an impact that we cannot see all enable us to plan more effectively. How you bring planning into your training sessions will depend on the purpose of your session.

Many of the interviewees considered this a crucial part of their training. Samara said, 'I'm in a very action-oriented, doing world, and it's important that they walk out with something to do.' And David spoke for many of us when he said how important it was to ensure relevance and give people thinking time to develop their plans, whether how to phrase specific emails, getting everyone contributing at team meetings or how to engage a different market or community with products or services.

Giving people thinking time, personally or in relevant groups, and ensuring people are taking away some record of their plan, is an important part of helping participants feel they are taking away something concrete. If you are working with a group across multiple sessions, build in a process to share the plans and return to them in future sessions.

The CQ Strategy element is Samara's favourite, as she can facilitate scenario planning or troubleshooting with her groups. People can think through and plan for what their options are in different scenarios in a training context, which is typically not tense. Practising in a context where emotions are not running high can lay down memories for people to draw from in the future.

Part of your planning as the trainer is thinking about the groups and purpose of your training and how you can best enable the group to plan. You can be creative. I have occasionally created scenarios and used role play and I've seen acting used to good effect by others as a medium for people to think through different options for planning how to respond.

I've been working with Afshan Baksh, a Lego Serious Play facilitator, to deliver 'Cultural Intelligence with Lego Serious Play' workshops on the theme of inclusion and have been delighted to see how the creative approach of using Lego draws everyone into the planning process. The way everyone contributes to the process is a key piece of feedback we get, including that it has been ideal for a participant who was not comfortable with eye contact and this creative approach had enabled them to fully participate in the planning process.

There are many ways to work with your participants to help them plan; two crucial ingredients are good questions and giving time. If you have a group from one organisation, with their goals and purpose established before you start, then it is often obvious which plans to focus on. If you have participants from many organisations, then options could be to create groups to establish common issues to focus a discussion on, or to use case studies. An important element I discovered over the years is that if a case study stops midway through a scenario and the question is 'Create a plan for what should happen now', then people can flex their noticing, assumptions and planning capabilities.

I've never been in a training room where everyone agreed on what should happen next. It instantly demonstrates how complex planning is when you are doing it with others. There is often no right and wrong, but better or worse and different impacts for different people. Opening up these potential impacts enables people to see that taking time to plan reduces the potential for negative impacts.

CQ Strategy is about how well we can use our knowledge and awareness to build plans that are fit for the contexts we operate in and the people we interact with. As a trainer, a large part of this is how you design your training to engage the people in the contexts they are in.

Checking

Planning is thinking through the options of how we influence, lead, communicate and interact with people. Part of the planning process is creating ways to check that what we are doing is working and having the intended impact.

While working with leaders, and generally in the West, I often find that reflection is an activity that is often struck off the to-do list. It is given a low value, or approached as little more than a tick list. Reflection is thinking with purpose, and it is crucial for learning and self-development. Without it, how will you, or anyone, know if they are developing their cultural intelligence? How will people know if their plans are working? If I'm working with people who like to tick actions off their checklist, or create peer groups for the purpose of reflecting with others, I sometimes recommend that reflection goes onto a to-do list.

Reflections are an important aspect of training. If you are running multiple sessions, starting with reflections about what has changed from the previous session can be a powerful way of enabling everyone to see what is changing for each participant.

One leader shared that he changed the end of his team meetings. Rather than saying something along the lines of 'OK, do we all know what we are doing and are good to go?', he switched to a round of checking what people had understood their priority was. He was incredulous that this substantially cut down what he described as 'firefighting' later in the week when people were doing something he couldn't understand. The time taken for checking understanding (in his international team) as part of the meeting meant that he was able to address different understandings in advance of people taking action and found that it saved time overall and led to smoother operations.

A useful checking approach, especially if it's about a scenario where you found interactions difficult, is reframing. Reframing is about stepping back and looking from a different perspective. I find one of the assumptions of appreciative inquiry useful. It asks us to assume everyone acts with good intentions. This doesn't mean that the good intentions are directed towards you. When I cannot understand someone's behaviour, or feel it has been negative, I find thinking through the question 'What were their good intentions?' to be a useful exercise. It invariably gets me thinking about relationships that are not to do with me but would be important to the other person, and I always find this calming in a way that enables me to reframe and plan a way forward.

The potential for checking can range from in the moment during interactions to decisions on what data needs to be gathered and how it is going to be collected in order to get an organisational picture. As a trainer, how do you check in the moment during interactions and afterwards that your training has delivered its intentions? And have you modelled cultural intelligence?

There are two questions I recommend for checking on your own interactions during training:

- What did you do well?
- What would you do differently if you were in that situation again?

When I'm coaching and mentoring, I notice that people often want to focus only on the problems. You need to know what you do well so that you can keep doing it and leveraging it. In order to share with participants, you also need to be aware of what has worked well for you, so you can share that. Sharing and noticing what you and others do well promotes a sense of value and worth.

There are always aspects of conversations or training that you could have done better or just differently. Did people understand your instructions? Was there tension in the group? How did you respond? Did you tell a story or joke that no one responded to? Do you wish you had responded to a question differently?

I have notebooks full of reflections on these questions, made after my training and coaching sessions. Research suggests that writing does help us lay down memory more than typing (Bendix 2024). Thinking through what you would do differently (rather than rebuking yourself for what you did wrong) is part of laying down plans for how you interact in the future. I'm looking for a good substitute for writing in notebooks as I now find writing difficult due to multiple sclerosis – and can confirm that for me, so far, I've not come across a process as useful as writing.

Noticing culture

Catherine says that three or four weeks into a course that is explicitly about CQ and having seen a film that is clearly cross-cultural, many of her students do not notice or comment on cultural aspects when asked to write down what they see going on in the film. This is the muscle, the habit, of looking for how culture is playing a part and factoring it into your understanding and planning. This habit, if it isn't there with your participants, cannot be developed in one training session. It takes time.

This is one of the reasons why my preference when working with companies and organisations is to have several shorter sessions rather than one longer one, and/or to build in individual or group coaching. It means you can build in reflection and noticing tasks between sessions to encourage people to build the habit of noticing culture. As well as taking the time, it can be useful to ask what people have taken away from a round of reflections. Noticing the value that you get from an activity is part of what motivates you to do it again.

We are all human. We are all shaped by culture. CQ Strategy is about being aware and noticing that, planning for what that may mean in the context you are in, and checking that those plans are working and your interactions are creating the impact you want them to. Without taking the time to develop this capability you, and your participants, will always be reactive rather than proactively engaging with people with cultural intelligence.

Key takeaways

✧ CQ Strategy cannot be developed in one event. It is about building a habit. Therefore, enable participants to make plans to build this habit.

✧ When we react and when we make plans, we do so more effectively when we are mindful of the assumptions we have and take the time to check them.

✧ As a trainer, CQ Strategy is a crucial aspect for designing training that engages the people you will be working with. It is useful to design with flexibility in mind (and decide what is high or low priority) so that you can respond to the people you are working with and expand or reduce or do something differently if you need to. When delivering your training, keep noticing and checking how others (and you) are reacting, and adjust your plans if necessary.

✧ You need to pivot between responding to each individual and creating a group dynamic where people can learn together. As a trainer, you are responding to individuals while communicating with the group.

✧ CQ Strategy enables you to be intentional and proactive rather than reactive when working with people from different cultural backgrounds.

Questions to consider

Before delivering training, alongside your planning, ask yourself questions to build awareness of your expectations about the group you will be working with:

✧ Who is in the room?

✧ What do I know and what do I not know (roles, relationships, stress levels, etc)?

✧ How am I feeling? What emotions and expectations am I taking into the training?

✧ What are my expectations of what they may think of me?

And during ...

✧ Are the participants engaging in different ways?
✧ How are energy levels/mood/interactions between participants? Do I need to address any of that?
✧ What is making me feel or respond this way?

And after ...

✧ What was unexpected?
✧ What did I do well?
✧ What would I do differently if I was doing that again? (For example, facilitating an exercise, answering a question, whatever aspect you think could have been done better, or just differently.)

Chapter 8

Developing CQ Action

I want participants to go being ready to listen to others, being ready to engage with others and... have the ability to think with a learner mindset and make mistakes. That's cultural intelligence. You cannot venture out into the world without being ready to make mistakes. – Anindita Banerjee

CQ Action is about being able to adapt your behaviours to communicate effectively, interact well with others and develop the relationships that are important to you. Being interviewed is an example of a time when we want our behaviours to be perceived positively. When I was at school, I was taught that at the beginning of an interview you should offer your hand for a quick, firm handshake while looking the other person in the eye. I have a memory of being told that people would think I was weak if my handshake wasn't firm and dishonest if I didn't look people in the eye.

I didn't need to interview many international students when I was in my twenties to learn that neither the quick, firm handshake nor eye contact are universal interview behaviours. When interviewing Nigerian students, for example, I'd hold out my hand to shake theirs and they would hold on. I'm aware that, at first, my discomfort overwhelmed me and all I'd be able to think about was my hand. Was it sweating? Could I yank it free? Yet we would find ourselves, hands free, seated at the interview table.

Touch was not a big part of our norms where I'm from in the north-east of Scotland. What I reflect on is that over time I have become comfortable with an extended handshake and can now hear and communicate during it. We can extend our comfort zones. I also recall that before my comfort zone expanded, I was so uncomfortable that I stopped hearing. I suspect the other person had no idea. Never forget that without intention, your actions could make someone so uncomfortable that they can no longer hear. This is a useful thought to keep front of mind when training (and in life generally).

Sometimes we don't even know that a behaviour is typical somewhere in the world. The first time I interviewed someone who didn't once look me in the eye, I struggled with my concentration, listening and speaking. I didn't even know that not establishing eye contact was a sign of being respectful in some places, nor that for some neurodivergent people establishing or maintaining eye contact can be a struggle.

I was unconsciously incompetent. If you think of the learning steps, you want to step up from unconsciously incompetent through consciously incompetent to consciously competent, and if you get there, to being unconsciously competent.

The three sub-dimensions of CQ Action listed in a CQ assessment are:

1. Speech acts – the words we use.
2. Verbal communication – how we say those words: pace, tone, volume, etc.
3. Non-verbal communication – everything your body does, except voice: facial expression, gestures, touch, spacing, etc.

In response to the question about which CQ capability has been hardest to develop, CQ Action topped the list for the interviewees, and all aspects of the three sub-dimensions were mentioned in terms of how hard it was, or had been, to behave against their norms.

This chapter considers the three sub-dimensions you get

feedback on as part of a CQ assessment, thoughts on delivering training to support the development of the CQ Action capability and suggestions to help you develop and use your CQ Action. Each of these sections is brief, yet each could be a book in itself as there are so many variables. The next chapter focuses on questions and listening – two key actions you must take into any training and which speak to Anindita's hope that you will be ready to listen and engage. This chapter has a focus on individual behaviours and Chapter 10 considers how the CQ framework can be used in training to support larger group change.

Speech acts

Andrej shared that, growing up in the former communist Eastern Bloc, he learned to avoid direct statements and code his messages. Conveying what he wanted to say in an indirect way was the norm. He quickly came to realise, when working in an international sales management role for a company headquartered in the US, that his indirect approach to communication meant that his messages got lost.

He said, 'In sales, you provide performance feedback on an almost daily basis. Whenever I had to give negative feedback to some of my team members, I did it in a very diplomatic manner. While some members of my team highly appreciated my communication style, others completely misunderstood my criticism and left the meeting room excited about how pleased their manager was with their performance. So, relatively early in my professional career, I learned that I needed to equip myself with a variety of communication styles and use them accordingly, otherwise I wouldn't go far in an organisation that was very diverse. I never lost my comfort with the nuanced, diplomatic and indirect way of conveying my messages, but regular practice helped me find comfort in more direct communication as well.'

Generally, the more culturally diverse a group, be that in terms of languages spoken or cultures experienced, the more you need to be explicit in your communication during training. It is easy to write 'be explicit in your communication' along with recommen-dations such as 'refrain from using metaphors', but it is less easy to do so. As Andrej says, he had to practise.

A metaphor is when a word is used in a way that is not its literal meaning. Metaphors grow out of a shared culture, making it hard for them to be understood across cultures (where they are frequently formed with simple words so that misinterpretations are easily created) and hard to recognise when you are within the culture that uses them as the metaphorical meaning is shared. 'It's a piece of cake' is used to mean something is easy in the UK, not that there is any cake involved. Does it make sense where you are?

Many words in English also have different meanings, which can add to linguistic confusion. When meeting international students who would tell me what university or city in Scotland they were studying and living in I would often ask, 'And how are you finding it?' There would be a pause, then a story about internet searches or education fairs that had led to the selected destination, or tales of how they had travelled. It took me a while to realise my question was using the word 'finding' in a different sense from how they were understanding it and I needed to switch to something like, 'What has your experience there been like so far?'

When you are in a one-to-one conversation, it can be easier to spot where your words are causing confusion. In group settings, that can be harder. I smile and shudder when I think about how often I have been in rooms of international students trying to get the technology to cooperate at the start of sessions, and looked up and said, 'Bear with me.' I suspect someone has heard 'Bare with me' and been stressed by my suggestion, or wondered, 'Where is the bear?' What I was trying to say was, 'Please be patient, I won't be long.'

The benefit of thinking through what words really mean is that you can deliver more impactful training to any group. This is especially important with international groups and groups where there is neurodiversity. When Zanne Gaynor and Kathryn Alevizos published *Is that Clear? Effective communication in a multilingual world* (2019), the tips were so useful for people with autism that they were encouraged to write another book angled at giving tips to enable effective communication in a neurodiverse world (2020).

Words your participants regularly hear and say, such as 'yes', are understood from different cultural perspectives. Take time to explore the potential meanings of words in the contexts you and your participants work in. Or think about how words translate from one language and culture into another, as this is frequently eye opening. I've witnessed how exploring that 'yes' can have a range of meanings, including 'I agree', 'Yes, I have heard you' and even 'Maybe'. This has led to people reinterpreting scenarios they have been part of. Reinterpreting leads to options for different actions they could have taken, or will take in the future.

How direct, how much context is shared, how politeness is demonstrated, whether questions are used to open up or shut down conversations, metaphors, idioms, acronyms and which subjects are deemed OK to talk about or are taboo are all aspects of speech acts.

Verbal communication

I am aware that over the years of working with people from all around the world, the pace of my speech has slowed down, and not just when I'm working with multilingual groups. I recall delivering CQ training to UK-based leaders in an international company that had international staff, and during one of the sessions a Chinese participant said he appreciated the pace and being able to understand everything. A colleague started to query this and the group realised that the many virtual discussions with UK colleagues speaking at pace in multiple regional accents resulted some of their international staff feeling that they had not fully comprehended the discussions, and this in turn was a factor in whether or not they contributed. Concern about being patronising if they slowed down, along with habits of speech, had stopped anyone checking.

The focus of meetings can often be about getting through the agenda rather than checking that everyone is following the discussion. As a trainer, you want to ensure that how you deliver your speech can be understood by all. While I've also had feedback that individuals have found my pace too slow, in this case what is more important is the group understanding rather than individual preferences. While it's never comfortable to read that someone did not appreciate an aspect of your training style, it has always been when I'm with groups with an international mix but the majority have overwhelmingly had English as a first language. You want to include everyone, which may well mean that you are not talking in the style most preferred by some. I do view feedback like this as a failure on my part, as it suggests that people have left thinking 'How would I have preferred this to be?' rather than 'What worked well for the group?', which seems central to being culturally intelligent.

I'm aware that in a training room there are certain verbal behaviours that can impact on my feeling anxious as I worry I'm not going to be able to hear and understand, such as when someone is very quiet or has an unfamiliar accent I find hard to decipher. I've taught myself to take a slow breath and focus, and nine times out of ten that extra focus does enable me to hear. On the other side, when volume is very loud, I used to feel I was being shouted at rather than focusing on just listening to the words. People can be loud for all sorts of reasons, ranging from being hard of hearing to being from large families where you had to shout to be heard, or being from cultures where volume was encouraged for reasons such as demonstrating to others that you are not talking about them.

As a Brit working with international groups, one of the key aspects of verbal communication I have to be aware of is tone. I can say 'That is interesting' and I could mean it as sincere, a joke or an insult depending on my tone (and perhaps facial expression). For someone not from the UK, that can be really hard to pick up on, and when I started working with international students it took me a while to use words literally rather than culturally (or to ensure that when they were used culturally they were being clearly explained).

The use of tone in this way is similar to Andrej's experience of using coded words. It is a way of communicating that only those 'in the know' would understand, which enables two messages to be conveyed at once to different audiences. I am not an academic who has knowledge of how and why speech patterns developed, but I can think of many from our history as to why that may have been useful here in Scotland.

In today's workplace, where so much of our communication is written, tone is an element that is always missing. I have found this to be a useful conversation when I'm working with groups in the UK where people speak of writing or reading emails with tone in mind. I may hear 'They should have known it was light hearted', which leads to useful conversations around how someone would know and what could have been written instead. Taking time to think about what may lie behind a style of verbal communication can be helpful for enabling people to let go of habits and be tolerant and accepting of different approaches.

Non-verbal communication

Fenny talked about how she pays attention to body language in her groups. She works with different groups, often a mix of American and Asian, and one of her observations is difference in body language when people disagree with her or have questions. When she sees someone leaning forward and looking at her, she often invites that person to share their thoughts making her invitation from the front so that everyone can hear. Alternatively, when someone (or groups) lean back with eyes down, she may go over and hunker down to their level to ask quietly what thoughts and questions they have. She is sensitive to this, especially when in mixed national groups, as expectations around sharing your voice, disagreement and how to interact with your facilitator are different.

Some interviewees shared reflections on how hard it was for them to behave against their non-verbal norms. One said that if they get feedback about how they kept their emotions hidden during difficult conversations in the room, they take that as a win as it is so difficult for them, but they know that during specific scenarios that's what is needed in order for the participants to share without feeling judged. As a trainer in this field, you will often have conversations that are sensitive or difficult, and being able to hear what people need to share without sharing your emotions about it through your body can be a challenge if you are expressive – or indeed vice versa.

It can be hard to know how to interpret other people's body language or indeed to know how others may be interpreting your facial expressions and body movements. One of the things I learned early in my training experience was that I can't read a person in terms of their engagement by relying on sweeping stereotypes about what different body language means, which I've 'learned' over the years.

I once trained a group of science communicators in Scotland who were going to be working with science communicators in Abu Dhabi. When we were in group sessions, which I was leading, one of the participants frequently had her arms crossed, looking out of the windows. My interpretation was that I was failing to engage her and she wasn't interested. At the end, she asked the most insightful questions, which made me realise I had misinterpreted her body language. Several months later, she commissioned me for similar but different work. I have learned that we can't tell without checking what body language may mean. The more culturally diverse the group, the more true this is.

One of the features of virtual training is that you see such a small part of a person and less interaction going on between everyone, which can make picking up on group dynamics more challenging as there are fewer non-verbal communication cues on display. You can pick up a lot about a group from how people interact with each other in a physical space. This is much reduced in the virtual world, where typically only one person is speaking at a time. There may, of course, be multiple private chats going on via messaging. While you would notice conversations in a physical space, messaging in the virtual environment is typically hidden from you.

In the virtual world, another key behaviour is the choice as to whether or not a participant switches on their camera. Some interviewees spoke about how hard they found talking to their screen with no faces looking back. Andrej's philosophy is that training is an invitation. Therefore you can invite people to switch their cameras on (especially in breakout room discussions) and have a discussion with the group about preferences and impact. However, on occasion, I was not the only one to have had the experience of feeling I was with a group who weren't really there!

It is always useful to share expectations in advance, and also to accept that some people are going to get more from the training if they keep their camera switched off. Investing in a standing desk was helpful for me, so I always deliver virtual training on my feet, which helps me to stay focused and keep my energy up regardless of whether participants have their cameras switched on or not.

As one of the interviewees said, how they respond to behaviours they find difficult often depends on how they themselves are feeling. This in turn reminds them to always hold that the choices of participants are theirs to make and that there are probably good reasons for them acting as they are.

Thoughts on effective CQ Action training

Whether you are providing a short training session, creating a long programme with features such as job shadowing or supporting an immersive experience such as a relocation, planning for how to enable people to expand their CQ Action capability involves creating (or reflecting on) scenarios for them to build awareness about their norms, the potential discomfort of developing new behaviours and engaging their hope that they will be able to do so.

Each of us has spent years developing our ways of communicating and doing things, and a key idea that I want you (and your participants) to take away is that change can be hard, even when you really want to change. Be kind to yourself. Be kind to others. Charles Duhigg wrote in his book, *The Power of Habit* (2012), 'Transforming a habit isn't necessarily easy or quick. It isn't always simple. But it is possible.'

I've worked with CQ trainers who spend very little time on the

CQ Action capability during their training, saying that if people get the knowledge and strategy and they have the drive, they know what to go and do. It's fairly easy to know something (and it's even easier to think you know what someone else should do), but even when we really want to do something differently it can be hard at an individual level and even more so at an organisational level. When you are within organisations, there is a culture of how things get done (whether that is effective for achieving goals or not). Taking the time to notice that culture, to recognise what barriers are getting in the way of positive impact and decision making, is rarely an easy task.

Therefore three important elements of CQ Action development are practice, support and accountability. These could be encouraged by how you design your programme, be that through getting participants to practise different behaviours (do they recognise the discomfort when it is not their norm?), running training events that include reflections about changes and/or the barriers to implementing change, providing individual or peer group coaching, or having your participants design a model of support and accountability that will work for them in their context.

During training, create short exercises that enable people to recognise the feeling of doing something outside their norm. That could be as short and simple as the arm fold exercise in Chapter 3, having a conversation while standing near or far, establishing eye contact or not, or creating scenarios and role-playing requests in a direct or indirect style, for example. The key is exploring the context and aims of your participants and being creative in how you suggest ways for them to notice their norms and practise new approaches.

For example, I've worked with organisations in the UK that have collaborations in various Arab countries. There is often a worry expressed by some of the men in the UK groups that they will cause offence by trying to shake hands across genders. Going through a process of thinking through what they will do instead has resulted in people deciding they will touch their heart or their shoulder, which gives an action (in part mimicking reaching out a hand to shake) which reduces the stress people feel. Reducing this stress is important as it can get in the way of listening and building rapport.

A useful exercise can be to create lists of 'what to do instead' from the taboos people have about working with other cultures, whether at a national level with a country a group are working with, conducting home visits across their community as part of a work role or with a demographic group in their organisation. It is much easier to follow through with an action when you tell yourself what you are going to do rather than being told to stop a behaviour that is familiar, easy and comfortable for you.

If I ask you not to think of a pink elephant, what are you thinking about? Typically, the instruction leads to thoughts of a pink elephant! The problem with lists of 'do nots' and taboos is that it puts the thought in your head. Don't dismiss the lists, but add another list of what to do instead.

Sometimes CQ trainers are asked what the difference is between the sociolinguistic sub-dimension in CQ Knowledge and CQ Action. Sociolinguistic knowledge is about knowing the rules of language in a given context, whereas CQ Action is about being able to change your communication behaviours to adapt to different rules or preferences.

As a trainer, what you focus on again depends on the purpose of your training. Three examples of themes my training have focused on are:

- academics seeking to build relationships with business
- a company developing a base in a country new to them
- women seeking to be heard more and have a sense of being taken seriously (in different country contexts).

All required a different emphasis, and they also required consideration around what communication norms typically were, what was working, what the challenges were and suggestions of which changes could help – then practising that, as to do things differently often means to feel uncomfortable at the start. This might be talking in the first rather than the third person; asking open rather than yes/no questions of colleagues when their opinion was being sought; or not starting conversations with the word 'sorry'. These suggestions came up in the three examples given. I am not suggesting they are always relevant to each theme and definitely not in all contexts. They were areas to practise, which came out of specific, focused conversations around communication and impact in each specific context.

In these scenarios the participants had arrived at changes they believed would result in more effective interactions through facilitated discussions. A couple of interviewees also shared an experience I have had, which is that people just want you to tell them what to do. 'We have paid you to train us. Tell us what to do!' is what one interviewee has experienced being told.

The idea that you can create a behaviour rule for all situations and for all people in a group is something that cultural intelligence training is trying to avoid. David has become known for saying, 'It depends'. And it is true. There are so many factors contributing to the complexity of our interactions. For example, in her book *Hysterical: Exploding the myths of gendered emotions* (2022), Praga Agarwal explores how the same behaviours are judged differently whether displayed by men or women across many cultures. For some, this level of uncertainty will be unsettling. Work with your group to explore what their current behaviours are, relevant to the theme and purpose, how they are impacting and what could improve outcomes for them.

How you facilitate discussions about CQ Action depends not just on purpose and culture, but the training situation. Is the training a hybrid event, an in-person meeting, a virtual meeting, a number of interactions over time or a one-off? These aspects will often help you focus on where to concentrate attention or which questions will most usefully enable your participants to explore what and when to change about their actions. As with CQ Strategy, the potential for scenario planning and role play can be useful for building muscle memory of options and communication approaches that could be utilised in the scenarios your participants encounter.

Developing and using your CQ Action

As trainers, we are all judged by our actions. In any training or coaching room, our actions will lead to participants deciding if we are culturally intelligent or not. If we are delivering training that includes cultural intelligence we want to be modelling what that can look like, otherwise it can undermine our purpose. We also need to keep an invitation open to participants to reflect on how they could think about behaviours differently.

It can be useful to have a constructive critical friend who can observe your training and give feedback on what you do to communicate well, what you are doing that is or could be confusing, or what could be more impactful. If you can team up with people from different backgrounds and/or who speak different languages, you can enrich that feedback. Alternatively, film yourself talking about an element of CQ. Many of us hate watching ourselves on film or hearing ourselves speak, but it is a great way of becoming familiar with our way of communicating. Ask yourself what you do well and what you could change to enable more people to learn, engage and be inspired by your training.

You may be working in many cultural contexts that you are not familiar with. As Anindita said, you need to plan and prepare and be ready to make and own your mistakes. You can also invite your participants to notice your behaviours and how they are influencing them. Can they remember how you opened the session (purpose, human connection, concepts – see Chapter 3)? How did it fit with their cultural expectations? If you sit informally on a table, how will that be perceived? You could have fun with some groups in terms of what they notice and think is culturally appropriate about your behaviours, while other groups would not engage with an activity that may be perceived as being critical of you.

The tension between being authentic and doing what will be most effective in the context was spoken about by a few of the interviewees, with one sharing that as they aged, this tension between adapting to behavioural norms and being authentic to themselves was increasing.

A tip shared by some interviewees was to share aspects of their communication and delivery style upfront so that people know what to expect, rather than focus on trying to change them. For example, some interviewees conduct training in languages that are not their first language. Some felt that this meant they had more verbal tics (umming and erring, for example), so they would state this upfront. This is a good strategy, but only if it enables people to understand, relate and engage with you. If you speak quickly in a way that prevents people from understanding you, then slow down. Toastmasters (toastmasters.com), the international public speaking organisation, is a super useful resource for trainers. They call the umming and erring 'filler sounds', and when you speak at one of their training events, it is someone's role to recognise and count the ones you use! This feedback focuses awareness and their structure facilitates improvement in everything related to speaking publicly, which is a crucial aspect of delivering effective training.

The interviewees spoke about paying attention to the mood, words and interactions of the people they are training. Which words are important to them? How do they interact with each other? This can give you clues as to what could serve you well with them and also highlight behaviours that are not serving them well in regard to their aspirations. It can sometimes be difficult to highlight behaviours and communication patterns that seem negative to a group. One way I find useful is to just state, 'I observe... [followed by what you heard or witnessed]. Tell me about that.'

Some interviewees spoke about the worry of expressing their emotions to participants during conversations that they found hard and were feeling negative about. A tip can be to think about what you do want to convey – for example, warmth and interest. Think through what this could look like in terms of your body language and be prepared to share it.

Rather than tell yourself that you won't be expressive in ways that show you are horrified, appalled or irritated (or whatever emotions you feel you would rather not share), tell yourself that you will have the expression of calm, of acceptance or warmth, or whatever range works for you and practise that expression at different, non-pressured times. What does it feel like? Pay attention to what is going on in your body so that you can replicate it, as calling on calmness when you are anxious is hard – especially if you don't know how that feels for you. A long breath helps with this, so that I'm not reacting and showing my emotion; I'm steadying myself in order to express calm.

A few interviewees spoke about situations where participants were trying to make them say something they felt it was best to leave unsaid – for example, a participant airing a grievance about management and wanting the trainer to agree with a specific perspective. Whether the person is justified or not and whether you agree or not is less the issue than what you are communicating to the group. A group is comprised of people whose individual perspectives you don't know. The interviewees spoke of treading that line of letting people know they were being heard and letting them know that they were there for a specific purpose, with the invitation to return to that purpose, all the while using their CQ Strategy to plan carefully and choose which words to share.

What happens when you encounter behaviours that challenge you?

The fight-or-flight response can often kick in and you can try to shut down the discussion or move things on. However, if there is something causing you discomfort, there is often an opportunity to learn something. It can be an opportunity to lean in and explore. Alternatively, sometimes we don't reflect and think about our behaviours and project judgement outwards if there is a misunderstanding. An irritated 'They weren't paying attention' is a regular comment I hear from trainers. I've felt it myself. Changing the focus to where you have agency can help shift this judgement, with questions such as, 'How can I get attention? Will there be a better time for this message? Do people need to attend to something else?'

We need to accept people as they are during training, while highlighting and creating invitation for people to expand their comfort zones and ways of communicating in order to be more effective and inclusive across cultures.

Questions that are explored in Chapter 11 related to CQ Action are:

- Who should adapt?
- How can you be authentic if you are always adapting to the cultural norms of others?

These questions are useful to explore, both with your participants and also to examine your own thoughts and flexibility when going into training.

- What aspects of your communication behaviours are you open to adapting?
- What could only be done with difficulty by you?

Catherine said: 'The point of cultural intelligence is to build better connections with other people so we like each other more and then we will work better together. Think of all the positive things that come from having deeper and higher quality connections.'

It's impossible to consider all possible variables when it comes to communication, and what I notice is that while my range, ability to flex and my patience have expanded over the years, I still make mistakes. How would it be possible not to? However, as I've become more culturally intelligent, I'm aware that I'm more likely to notice when I'm making a mistake with a person or group. I'm also more likely to react by thinking 'What could I do differently?' rather than judging the behaviour of others. None of us can be all things to all people all of the time. What you can do is build your awareness of noticing when you are not being understood, or getting engagement and building your strategies and practising the behaviours for responding to that in the contexts you operate in.

Key takeaways

✧ Knowing what we, or others, should do is the easy part. We spend decades developing our habits, so changing them can be uncomfortable. Acknowledge this.

✧ Changing our behaviour typically takes practice in order to expand our comfort zones.

✧ The range of communication behaviours is vast. We cannot possibly master everything, but we can be more attuned to when we are not having the effect we hoped for. This is an opportunity to lean in and learn.

✧ We only have agency over our own actions, as do our participants. That is the only useful place to focus – where we have agency.

Questions to consider

✧ On reflection, how could a change in your communication and delivery style have improved engagement with a specific group?

✧ Do you have repeat scenarios where people in your training do not understand, do not engage or talk over each other? (Insert the scenario that best describes some behaviours in your training that you consider less than ideal.)

✧ How would you describe your behaviours during that scenario?

✧ What could/will you try to do differently in the future?

✧ Which behaviours from participants can cause you anxiety or irritation, or are ones that you gravitate towards?

✧ How does that feeling impact on your behaviours?

Chapter 9

Questioning and listening

I listen carefully because they are telling me who they are, what matters to them, telling me how they perceive me through their norms, through their standards... And that helps me to build knowledge about a person so I can start planning for bridging the difference, if there is any.
– Andrej Juriga

The act of asking questions influences the direction people, organisations and communities take, which makes good questions crucial for developing ourselves and others. The art of asking good questions is rooted in listening well.

David said that he saw how listening cut across all the CQ capabilities. He would sometimes want to slow down someone's CQ Drive and encourage them to go forward as a listener, with some humility. CQ Drive could also create that drive to want to listen. Without listening, he asked, how could we build CQ Knowledge and CQ Strategy? I agree that listening impacts our ability to enhance each of the CQ capabilities and I think of it as part of CQ Action.

Listening is an element I believe is missing from the CQ assessment and development language. It seems to me to be such an essential part of relating and working effectively across cultural difference – yet it is not explicitly mentioned. The questions you ask and the way you listen are key for developing people.

To me, this means you have a responsibility to keep expanding your ability to ask questions that support people to thrive, grow, develop and interact constructively with each other. If you are not asking questions, I would suggest you are delivering a presentation rather than training. As cultural intelligence is about human interaction, lecturing is not an ideal way to enable development. In the book *A More Beautiful Question* (2014), journalist Warren Berger argues that asking better questions can improve decision making, spark creative problem solving, strengthen personal relationships and enhance leadership.

Most interviewees cited that developing coaching skills was the learning that supported them to be more effective cultural intelligence trainers. In coaching, listening and questioning are the tools you have to work with.

How we question and listen and to whom we address questions or listen are impacted by culture. This chapter shares information about questioning and listening for you to consider. There are questions and thoughts about listening throughout the book, with Chapter 7 about CQ Strategy being particularly relevant. Part of developing any skill is building awareness of your current practice. I would happily design entire courses about listening and/or the power of questions, and it is rare for me not to include some exploratory discussions and/or exercises to build people's awareness and ability to listen and question well.

The art of questions

There is an ART to questions. (With thanks to the British Council for their permission to share this acronym, which was used in their InterAction Leadership in Community Development programme, 2007–2010).

A is about the Aim

Are you clear about the purpose of the question (before you start asking, or answering)? Who will the answer be for – ie, is it for you or the recipient(s) of the question? I frequently have to hold back from asking curious questions when I'm with people who bring up topics that fascinate me and are about my areas of interest rather than the purpose of the conversation or training. I'm a sucker for ideas, but it's not always what is useful and it really isn't about me. When I'm with friends, or building friendships, then of course questions that highlight my various interests can be important, but not when I'm coaching and training.

- What is the impact you are trying to have?
- Are you hoping to open up a topic for exploration or close it down (or postpone)?

Being aware of the aim of your question is a useful way of developing the art of questioning.

R is about the Relationship

What is the relationship between you (or the questioner) and the recipient of the question? How long have you known each other? What is the history between you? In which roles? How much trust is there between you? (How do you know?)

- How might the relationship impact on how the question is heard?
- How might the relationship impact on how the recipient might be prepared to answer?
- How might the relationships between everyone who can hear the question impact on how it is answered?

T is about Timing

You know that you have a purpose, which is to ask a person a specific question. Take a moment to consider, is this the best time?

- What else is going on?
- Is the time right for them to hear the question?
- Is the time right for you to hear and engage with the response?

I suspect there is no such thing as a perfect time for anything, but there are definitely times that are better or worse.

When you are training across cultures, it can make considerations about the aim, relationship and timing more complex. Sometimes one of the most useful questions is the silent one you ask in your head about what is going on in a situation – using your CQ before reacting to a received question or crafting one to ask.

Different styles of questions – developing your art

There are many types of questions. Do you have a style of questioning? Do you use a variety of styles? What could you usefully develop and include to create different impact?

Here are some suggestions for you to consider:

1. Enabling people to establish meaning and the possibility of lots of different realities.

- What will your team be seeing and experiencing when you have more CQ Drive?
- What do you want us to understand from that comment?
- What meaning are you giving to this?

2. Connecting questions enable people to explore and connect with what is influencing them.

- What was your experience of working with your [last boss, for example] and how is it influencing you now?
- What has worked well for you in the past that could improve this situation?
- What was your purpose in having that conversation? Did you share that purpose with the others with whom you were having the conversation?

3. Encouraging perspective taking and considering options or events from different viewpoints.

- If you assume they meant well, what do you think they would say if you asked them what they hoped to achieve from this action?
- Putting yourself in your line manager's position, how might

they feel about what you have just said?

- What aspects of your work are your children most proud of?

4. Embedded suggestion questions, helping to make positive outcomes visible and therefore possible.

- How will your team benefit when you have invested time in developing your inclusive leadership?
- How will the organisation benefit when everyone enhances their cultural intelligence?
- What are the valuable contributions the new migrants will make to this town?

You would typically want the embedded suggestion to be a positive one.

5. Questions that give options.

A question that offers two options can be useful when time is short, or when narrowing down options. A common option question is one that carries the expectation of 'yes' or 'no' responses. I notice they are used regularly in contexts where speed and direct communication are valued. There are places where responding 'no' would not be typical, so be mindful of context and to whom you are directing the question (an illustration of this is in Chapter 2). As a trainer, it can also be useful to keep possibilities alive rather than have people think 'no'.

- A question such as 'Was this useful?' invites a 'yes' or 'no' response. If 'no' is the quick response, there is no further need for the participant to keep thinking about the topic.
- A question such as 'What was useful?' carries the assumption that something was useful. You will have planted a seed to get people thinking about what has been useful whether they give a verbal answer or not.

6. Constructing one simple question.

One thing I learned early on with the British Council (and yet I still fail to do this on occasion) was to ensure that I only asked one question at a time in mixed language groups.

'Will we carry on or do you want to explore this further?' These are two separate questions, yet it's an example of something I might say. When people are not hearing their first language, they may need more processing time and the chances are that combined questions can get lost, so do try to develop the habit of thinking about the key thing you want to ask and take small, clarifying steps.

Questioning 'Why?'

◆ Why did you decide to read this book?
◆ Why have you positioned yourself where you are to read it?
◆ Why did you choose that outfit today?

Have you answered these three questions? Think about how you phrased your responses. Did you use the word 'because' at, or near, the start of your responses? Or could you have slotted that word in without changing the meaning of your response?

When I'm working with groups, I often ask three 'why' questions (letting participants know that for this exercise I'm not overly interested in the answer so to not overthink it). When I then ask, 'Which word was used at the start of the responses?', most of the responders had used the word 'because'. That has happened both with British and international groups. (I've always used English as the language of delivery. Know the language patterns of your context.)

Asking everyone 'What are we doing when we say "because"?' elicits responses such as, 'We are explaining, or defending, or justifying ourselves.' As a coach, I was taught not to use questions that start with why, as once someone has justified themselves, they are much less likely to stay open minded or explore a situation. More often, they will keep defending their justification. In training rooms, where the approach is cultural intelligence supporting aspirations around themes such as change, inclusion, international effectiveness or leadership, you want people to keep a curious, open mindset.

All questions are useful sometimes. Repeatedly asking 'why'

questions can be a good way of getting below the surface and understanding the root cause of a problem, particularly when that problem is mechanical or to do with systems, such as the systems in the body, for example. They're not so great for understanding what is impacting work relationships and group dynamics.

Without a doubt, you want to know your purpose (your why) for doing things. Experience has taught me that 'why' questions are not the best route for getting there. This is not just true in a work context. As a mum to triplet boys, ditching questions such as 'Why did you do that?' (often asked in exasperation) in favour of questions starting with something like 'What were you doing before this happened?' created space for a different response, a conversation and better communication between us.

For example, you may want to know why research (Carter et al 2018) across 20 countries found that in academia, women asked fewer questions than men after seminars. This was amplified when the first question was asked by a male. However, asking the women why they ask fewer questions is unlikely to get you to a useful answer. I don't have the answers, and the behavioural science (Weingarten 2019) about who asks questions, when and why, is patchy. In Scotland, why and how are sometimes used interchangeably, so if you hear someone say 'How no?' it typically means you are being asked, 'Why not?' Therefore, as with all my suggestions, they all come with the caveat of knowing your context.

Practising questioning

During training, it can be useful to introduce different styles of questions that help people to explore a topic, and then invite them to practise in pairs – something along the lines of one to explore a topic with the other only using open questions (what, when, how, where, when and avoiding why). You can add the acronym TED:

- Tell me about...
- Explain more about...
- Describe more about...

It may be useful to pick an uncontroversial theme for the initial exercise (favourite food, holidays etc, which the individual can pick for themselves) and give time for a conversation. Then swap roles. When debriefing, I often discover that many people find it hard to use open questions. (I would not do an exercise like this with coaches – questions are their key tool so, as with everything, consider the audience.)

On the other side of the exercise, the participants being asked open questions typically felt they were being really listened to and heard. However, where there is distrust or a power play going on, being asked open questions can make people feel insecure; so the mantra is that you can never know enough about the people you are working with in order to design training that will be most useful for them.

As a trainer, aim to be observant in the spaces in which you work. Who is asking the questions? What impact is it having? How can you use questions for positive impact? Crafting good questions for participants to explore topics and scenarios is crucial for generating insights and starting useful discussions.

I have written on LinkedIn about the importance of questions for determining the direction that people may travel, and one of the responses gave me pause for thought. It said that this seemed like such a responsibility that it almost made them too nervous to ask questions. You are a trainer; you cannot avoid them. It is not possible to lead well, to be effective across cultures, to be inclusive, without the use of good questions. Pay attention to the questions you hear or are asked by others and gather the good ones. Which questions do you see having a positive impact on others? What was the context? Could you use that question?

Clean language

The clean language methodology was developed for use in clinical settings by David Grove, a psychologist from New Zealand, in the 1980s and 1990s. It is now used across many areas for those working with others. The aim is to keep your thoughts, assumptions and metaphors out of your questions. For example, if you ask 'Was that depressing for you?', you are projecting your assumption that it would be depressing. Instead, ask, 'How was that for you?' (see Clean Change nd).

Clean language is particularly useful when you are exploring a person's experience or feelings about something as it ensures people can use their words rather than reacting to the words they have been offered. When you are developing people, as per the suggestion earlier about embedded suggestion questions, you want to encourage optimism that people can improve their effectiveness across cultures. Sharing assumptions can be useful. The hope is that you will do so with awareness and know the intention of your questions.

The other side of developing your noticing of when language is being used cleanly is when you hear it in other people's questions, which gives you an opportunity to check, 'Am I hearing you have an assumption that...?' It contributes to showing that you are taking an interest and really listening.

Receiving questions and responses

I love questions. I'm frequently paying attention to how others construct them. Yet I rarely thank people for their questions. I notice, especially when working with American trainers, that when someone asks a question, there is often an affirmation ('great question') or thanks. This is a cultural difference I can then speak to and/or adapt to when in specific groups.

One of the questions I often hear when I'm training CQ facilitators is, 'How should I respond to a difficult question?' Each of us will have a different perspective of what a difficult question is, of course, but some thoughts are to:

- pause
- calm yourself
- clarify with a question ('Am I understanding that you are asking me...?')

- ask the questioner a question (eg 'What impact were you aiming to have on us all with this question?' or 'How does this relate to your cultural challenges?')
- ask the group what they think? ('Does anyone have experience they could share about this?')
- say you need time to consider that question and that you'll return to it, either for the group, or with the individual – whichever you say, do make sure you do
- know that if you can't answer the question, think about who you could ask to get information for the person afterwards (and offer it to the room if anyone else would find a response useful)
- ask them to remember the question and ask it again at a specified later point in the training
- keep your response brief if you are feeling unsure or anxious – some of us (I know I do) talk more when we are anxious, and it is not usually helpful.

Culture impacts on our expectations about who should ask questions, how they should be received and who should answer, as well as how we construct and use different types of questions. It can be useful to explicitly discuss this, as it helps to highlight if and what changes in approaches to using questions would best support the change needed with the people you are working with. Culture also impacts on our expectations of how the response will arrive. Getting comfortable with silence was a key for me being able to receive responses well. Give people time to hear and process.

I remember a conversation with a university participant who had been in Japan for meetings to discuss potential university collaborations. Her questions were met with silence. Rather than wait, she would keep talking as she did not have an awareness at that time that the priority in Japan tended to be thoughtful consideration of the question that requires a period of silence in which to construct a response. She said she left feeling humiliated as she had begun to speak incessantly. This was a great learning opportunity for her, one she fervently wished she had been aware of in advance of her trip.

If people are learning in a language that is not their dominant one, it can impact on how quickly people process a question and form a response.

What is your relationship with silence when you ask questions? If you are not comfortable with silence, a tip can be to give yourself something to do while you are being silent after asking a question. Count or recite a rhyme silently in your head, take a sip of water or focus on your breathing.

You may be working with people who prefer to answer on behalf of a group, or preparing people to receive and respond to questions in a different context to their norm, be that in business or as study abroad students. Whatever your purpose and group, pay attention so that you can notice and adapt how you deliver and receive questions, but also enable your participants to experience what it is like to expand their questioning repertoire.

Listening

Do you talk about developing capacity to listen in your CQ training? How, or where, do you link it with the CQ framework? I am aware that when my sons were at primary school, they would often have exercises to do at home that were about reading, writing or presenting. There were never exercises about listening. When I think back to my schooling, I have no memory of having listening lessons, except when learning a foreign language or musical notation. It is as though the belief is that listening is passive and will just happen. Yet the cultures we are surrounded by impact how we listen, when we listen and who we listen to.

Developing CQ Action contributes to you being better at what is known as active listening, which asks you to focus fully on the person speaking when you are listening, using your empathy to pay attention to verbal and non-verbal cues as well as the words. Understanding more about these clues in different cultures enables you to listen, understand and respond in ways that demonstrate interest and listening better in more cultural contexts.

There are so many excellent proverbs and quotes about

listening that you can use to generate discussion. Any group you work with will have examples of advice they have been given about listening, so you could invite people to share. One I like is a quote from Stephen Covey (2020): 'Most people do not listen with the intent to understand, they listen with the intent to reply.' I like this as I recognise myself in it and it often resonates with people I work with in the UK. Other feedback I have found useful to share was provided by African participants, from various countries, on a British Council leadership programme. 'British people don't really listen, they just jump in to solve.' Again, I recognise myself in this. Tell me your problem and before you have finished speaking, I'll have three potential solutions for you.

Offering solutions to problems typically comes from a good place. It is also a learned behaviour. When I mull on this, I hear the echoes of colonialism, knowing what is best for others. What does it make you think? I recognise it frequently when working with leaders in the UK and US, where much of my work is based. They are seeking to be more inclusive, yet are frequently unaware of how culture has shaped how they listen and what they listen out for. If we are to connect with people, we need to be listening.

There are some things that I'm aware have enhanced my listening. One was reading *Time to Think* (1999) by Nancy Kline, which is about creating thinking cultures. Her premise is that the quality of decisions depends on the quality of the thinking. For quality thinking, we need to be listening to each other. It sounds so basic, yet time after time I note that listening is not evident in the groups I'm working with or I'm aware that my mind has wandered and I'm not listening with full attention. I have found all of Kline's work helpful, and what I find galvanising, linked to the habit of listening to offer solutions, is that she writes that when you jump in to solve the problems shared with you, you are choosing to 'infantilise' those people, while listening and questioning would help to empower them.

The thought of infantilising others unnerves me. I had a visceral reaction to that and the thought has always stayed with me and contributed to enhancing my listening. I find this useful to share when I'm working with people who are talking about empowerment of staff and colleagues, yet they are not considering how they listen and how that contributes. 'I don't have time to listen' is a riposte I hear. 'When would you save time if you took the time to listen?' is a question I often respond with.

When I trained with the British Council as a trainer for their Intercultural Fluency programmes, they included exercises to consider how the words people use show us what is important to them. The four communication styles (Watson et al 1995) they encouraged us to listen out for are:

- action-orientated: a focus on solutions, what to do, practicalities, outcomes
- content-orientated: a focus on data, evidence, positive and negatives, discussion
- people-orientated: a focus on relationships, impact on people, beliefs, trust, morale
- time-orientated: a focus on time being well spent, realistic timeframes, concise messages.

Each of us probably has a couple of dominant preferences. It may shape how you design and deliver your training. It will have an impact on the words you use. Consider if your dominant styles are working with the audiences you are with. All cultural values and behavioural preferences have aspects of communication linked to them. Without listening with the intent to understand, you will miss the clues.

'What's your CQ?' is a participant guide that the Cultural Intelligence Center gives to participants of some of their CQ workshops. Against each of the ten behavioural preferences, it includes an example of people with this behavioural preference.

- For individualism (emphasis on individual goals and rights), it suggests, 'Say things like "I'll take care of this".
- For collectivism (emphasis on group goals and personal

relationships), it suggests, 'Say things like "Let me check with the team".'

It can be a useful exercise to expand on this with teams to consider the situations they are in. What are people hearing and how are they interpreting what they hear? For example, interviewers for organisations may well know that some have a cultural preference for 'we' over 'I'. A question such as 'What has changed in this team because of your impact?' could draw different responses from people with a strong preference for either individualism (I) or collectivism (we). What possibilities arise when they think of how this may be answered differently? Do they have a cultural preference? How will that impact on how they hear, interpret, respond and understand? Deep dives into the scenarios participants are involved in, what they hear and how they could consider hearing differently are useful discussions to facilitate.

I'm only too aware that I could often be much more attentive and craft far better questions, in part because so many aspects contribute to whether we are listening and what we are listening for. A consideration for you as a trainer is to listen and be attentive to yourself. What is going on in your head? Is it serving you well? Your capacity to listen well is reduced by emotions such as anxiety, stress and anger. You are human, so the chances are that you are going to experience these emotions during training (whether caused by technology, the behaviour of participants or events in your life outside your training work). I was never taught to listen well, but it is a skill I can intentionally develop. Listening takes energy. Are you using your energy to listen well? When you do, as Andrej said in the quote that starts this chapter, what is important to the other person is revealed. This in turn enables us to choose what will achieve the best impact in our communication.

Key takeaways

✧ Culture impacts who asks questions, how questions are constructed and how they are answered.

✧ Culture impacts on how we listen, what we listen for, to whom we listen and how we interpret both the words and the silences we hear.

✧ The act of asking questions can influence the way organisations and people can go. Keep reflecting on and improving your questioning.

Questions to consider

✧ How would you describe how your cultures have influenced how you use questions and listen?

✧ What could you learn and use from other cultures about questioning and listening?

✧ What advice, proverbs or quotes resonate with you about listening? When and how would they be useful to share in your training?

✧ What do you need to do to listen attentively?

✧ Do you develop listening and questioning skills with your participants to support developing CQ for your training themes and purpose?

Chapter 10

Using the capabilities together

It's easy to tell yourself or others what to do. It's quite hard to go through the process of the how. – Sandra Upton

The interviewees wanted to share and engage people with the CQ framework. It was seen as a crucial tool that people could take away to understand what was required to work well across cultures. It didn't matter where people were in terms of their capabilities; if they attained knowledge of the framework and were inspired to grow and apply it, they could keep layering in development and understanding of how they were building their strengths. CQ is like the systems of health and fitness – there isn't a quick-fix, one-size-fits-all approach: it's a constant endeavour with multiple factors at play.

Whether you are working with an individual, a group of unrelated individuals or intact teams, an important aspect of any training programme is to enable people to take something useful and practical away that enables them to apply their learning. Suggestions for that were using the CQ framework as a planning tool (as well as a development tool) and aligning CQ with other models and approaches that contributed to the impact being sought.

The four questions considered in this chapter are:

- Which capabilities should your participants focus on?
- How can they use the CQ framework as a practical tool?
- Are there other models that CQ aligns well with?
- How does context affect how you design your training?

Which capabilities should your participants focus on?

The four capabilities of CQ work together. There may be a capability more relevant or important for an individual person or group at a specific time, but each is important in the quest for cultural intelligence.

You have read that each of the interviewees has found different capabilities harder to develop or maintain, or they are aware that their perspective on which capability is most important has changed, or their assumptions about certain groups (such as leaders) have impacted on which capabilities they give weight to.

When creating training programmes, it can be useful to reflect on whether or not the emphasis you give to different capabilities is weighted in your experience (or indeed unchecked assumptions you have about your participants) or the CQ feedback, experience and purpose of your participants, keeping the invitation open for people to continue exploring how developing their capabilities could support them in their contexts.

For example, I know from both the research and my experience that each capability can be developed, yet I frequently hear from people (especially in coaching conversations) that they believe CQ Drive or CQ Action are just natural – ie you either have them or you don't. I was coaching an individual who had been promoted to a managerial role in the international office of a university in the UK. She batted off the feedback from her CQ assessment feedback report about her high CQ Drive and CQ Action as simply natural. As we explored further, she talked about how, on her trips to India for work, she had enjoyed the experience of not always knowing what to expect and adapting to unfolding situations.

This couldn't have been more different to how the new recruit (who had filled her previous role and whom she now managed) responded on her first trip. Annoyed by changing situations and dismayed by aspects of hosting and travel, the new appointee had sent messages of complaint to partners and hosts in India within a short time of arriving. This necessitated more senior engagement from the university having to address discontent on many sides.

Thinking of CQ Drive and CQ Action as simply natural meant an opportunity in advance of the trip to talk through not just tasks, but also expectations of being in this different culture and ways of responding to it had been missed. Knowing how uncomfortable difference may be for some is a crucial element of recognising part of the 'how' to adapt, as you can prepare them to expect this discomfort.

An example given to highlight the relevance of CQ Strategy came from a participant from a seminar one of the interviewees had been leading. The individual had implemented a whistleblowing system for their company that was working well in North America and Europe and they had led on expanding it to Asia. At no point during the rollout in Asia had they thought about culture, and in the end it was not successful. The Chinese didn't want to call an anonymous hotline to report on their boss, and while they received a lot of calls in India, they were not about serious misconduct. It was more about complaining about the boss as people thought it was a way to get to the bigger boss.

Another interviewee had said they had seen the train wreck when strategy was created without enough cultural knowledge, as the example above illustrates. This takes me back to earlier chapters when the interviewees were discussing what they wanted their participants to take away from any training, ie to start to see and recognise the impact of culture around them and have the CQ framework as a tool for navigating the complexity of culture.

It can be overwhelming to think of everything at once. Provide guidance and support that enables people to focus on what is most useful for them. Give them time, a useful question and an opportunity to debrief their plans.

- How are they leveraging their strengths?
- What could the impact of doing more of this be?
- Developing which capability would have the most impact for achieving their goals?
- What will be happening when they have developed that CQ capability that is different to now?
- What is a short-term and a long-term goal for developing your CQ?

Using the complete CQ framework

Imagine you are getting into the lift with the key decision maker and budget holder who decides whether or not there will be cultural intelligence training. You have two minutes to engage them with how developing CQ will contribute to improvements.

What are you going to say?

Go.

How did you go about that?

Did you craft a well-worded, inspiring statement?

Did you decide on some questions you could ask to find out what would resonate (in the hope of piquing interest and a later discussion)?

Did you disregard my request as a ridiculous notion that didn't give you nearly enough information to respond adequately to?

Or perhaps something else?

An exercise like this can be useful to get people thinking about making the case for cultural intelligence. Perhaps you are working with independent consultants or people who will have to make a case for training within their organisation. Working in pairs or groups with the aim of pitching for the benefits and purpose of investing in building CQ is often useful.

If the training is for intact teams and planning a project, a manager thinking about how to structure conversations they find difficult (or perhaps avoid) or an individual relocating, think about which questions will enable them to use CQ as a planning framework as well as an approach for personal development. This will enable people to apply CQ in a practical way to their challenges and opportunities.

Creating an exercise or a series of exercises that enable people to use the framework in a practical way to plan helps to embed any content and activities and crucially gives people something concrete to do as a consequence of the training. The simplest way is to give people planning time and a template with a series of questions that gives them a structure to use the CQ framework to plan. The first step is for people to have identified the challenge or opportunity they wish to address.

Here are some suggestions of questions to plan with cultural intelligence, but these are by no means the only ones.

CQ Drive

* What will better look like?
* What's your motivation for addressing this?
* What has worked well for you in the past?
* What are the expected benefits of this plan?
* How will you notice (or celebrate) improvement (or success)?

CQ Knowledge

* What do you know about what is impacting this situation?
* What role does (or will) culture play in this?
* What are our knowledge gaps (and should we, or how should we, fill them)?
* What do we know about our behavioural preferences? How is this showing up in our team?

CQ Strategy

* What are your assumptions (about the data, the people, the processes or systems; are there key aspects most relevant for your group to consider)?

- Who else do you need to speak to (or get different data and insights from)?
- What has not typically worked or had the impact you wanted? How can you reframe it to develop another approach using your CQ Knowledge?
- Will this plan have the desired impact on everyone in the organisation (community, company etc)? Are there groups we have not taken into consideration? What does this change?
- Create a plan (or operating guidelines, or strategies – whichever language works best) that uses the knowledge you have.
- What processes/strategies/people will you work with to check it is working?

CQ Action

- What are you going to commit to doing?
- How are you going to communicate about this plan or while implementing it? (Are different approaches required?)
- How will I (we) be held accountable?
- How will I (we) be supported?
- What needs to be practised?
- Which actions need to stop? What will they be replaced by or adapted to?

Instinctively, I often want to give people many questions and for them to choose which work best for them. (This gives clues about my preference for hierarchy, individualism and responding to uncertainty, to name some of the aspects of culture that may impact on such a decision.) I've learned that this causes confusion in most training situations, so if you are creating a planning template based on the CQ framework, craft one question for each quadrant that relates to the purpose of your training. The feedback is always that people appreciate the clarity of the questions as there is always complexity within the answers.

If you are running a programme with multiple sessions over a period of time, you will, no doubt, have many points at which you are setting goals, checking in and encouraging reflections on learning between sessions, along with developing the understanding of barriers or working through unexpected consequences. The 'how' is embedded in the context. Keep opening discussions that explore how you can build and apply your participants' CQ within the contexts they operate in.

Incorporating other approaches into your training

The focus of this book is cultural intelligence. Many of the interviewees sometimes, or always, use other approaches (to either amplify the potential to develop CQ capabilities, or to fuse approaches alongside CQ to better achieve their training purpose, such as leadership development) or frameworks (and use CQ as a lens for examining how to enhance the impact of those frameworks). This book is not going to examine those other approaches (that would require another book); however, questions similar to those below may be useful to explore before you start designing your training.

* Which frameworks are your participants using that CQ could amplify?
* What are the approaches that link with enhancing CQ?
* Where does CQ fit within the programme you are developing?

Draw from what clients are familiar with or using. For example, if you are addressing issues of conflict, what is the conflict resolution methodology being used and how can you fuse it with the lens of CQ?

The question of how the lens of CQ can amplify the impact of other frameworks and models is a useful one. Recruitment, communications, leadership development, decision-making processes – there is little at organisational level that doesn't have a process framework attached. Understanding these frameworks and thinking about how to use the CQ framework to enhance them is a great way of bringing CQ to life by working with an approach your trainees already use and that you can explicitly work through.

In her book *Building Inclusion* (2025), Marsha Ramroop creates questions for each of the CQ capabilities in order to improve inclusive behaviours at multiple points in the work cycle of architecture and built environment companies, including creating, attracting and retaining talent and engaging with communities. It's a useful resource for thinking through how you could use the CQ framework to provide support through the different aspects of creating, growing and sustaining an organisation.

None of the interviewees felt that cultural intelligence was the only capability people required to achieve the desired outcomes of the people they were working with. People are complex, organisations and communities even more so. Some would use CQ as the main approach, knowing that it is an agent for change in itself, drawing in other methodologies to enhance CQ (appreciative inquiry, mindfulness and cultural agility [see Meyer 2016] were tools and approaches that were each cited by at least three interviewees, which they would weave into training in order to amplify the capacity of trainees to build their CQ). Fenny said that when she was training in Asian countries, drawing from different models seemed to increase trust in her and the veracity of CQ, rather than when it was introduced in isolation.

John Kotter's methodology, eight steps for leading change, was the framework most often cited by the interviewees (Kotter 2006). They weaved CQ through this methodology to enhance international effectiveness and inclusion. The eight steps underpin three goals, which are to create the climate for change, engage and enable, then implement and sustain. Organisational change is culture change and therefore thinking of culture (and how to apply CQ) will elevate the chances of success at each of the points. There are, of course, many models of organisational change and CQ is always a useful framework to link them with. If you wish to link CQ with other models, then consider what your client (and of course yourself) are familiar with. Will it add or detract from your training purpose?

The lesson that I take from this is that, as a trainer, the commitment to keep developing yourself, learning and adding to your capabilities will serve you, and crucially the people you train, well. It will enable you to be more adaptable to the contexts in which you provide training. The tool most interviewees use to embed and enhance their training is a coaching approach, which enhances how they support people to build their CQ, whether during facilitated discussions, one-to-one coaching or peer group coaching.

The interviewees drew from the following approaches:

+ emotional intelligence (EQ)
+ appreciative inquiry
+ Kotter's change model
+ systems thinking
+ values-based leadership
+ decision-making models such as complex/complicated and/or urgent/important matrix
+ inclusive leadership
+ mindfulness
+ meditation
+ diversity, equity, inclusion, belonging – CQ development creates a space for conversations and actions around DEIB.

People, place, purpose and the time you have available are key to discussions about incorporating other frameworks and approaches into your training. You want your training programmes to be coherent and give your participants the confidence that they can leave with a concrete plan. Be clear about how you will link and take people through the elements you are introducing. If you do not have clarity about why you would link frameworks, then you may cause confusion. Remember that people can only absorb so much at one time.

Context and design

Fenny said that when she is working with Americans, she wants to get to the point quickly and keep managing time for everyone. It is accepted and expected that timings will be set for exercises and debriefing. Fenny's experience is that Singapore is very similar. People want input and content and think that the trainer is being paid to have answers. Whereas when she delivers training in China, Japan or South Korea, she is conscious of creating much more space for reflection and discussion to create meaning.

Colleagues who train in Europe and the US shared a similar experience. The expectation of the US audience can be to lots of content, delivered quickly, with timed interactive exercises and discussions, whereas European groups can prefer more time for conversation, creating meaning and debriefing. Justin, in Rwanda, spoke of the importance of creating space for storytelling.

Developing contacts who deliver training in contexts you will be working in is a great strategy for building your expectations and knowledge of what may work best in different places, whether they are different organisational types or different places in the world (alongside the discussions with people from any organisation you are going to be working in).

Wherever the interviewees were training, a key aspect that had changed with experience for many was the comfort of ignoring and adapting their plans and training schedule, reframing discussions and keeping them going when they recognised it was of importance, or adapting a style of exercise so that they could respond to the energy and reactions of the people they were working with.

Useful planning techniques to help you be adaptable during training sessions, if this is something you find hard, are:

1. Decide which aspects of your training design are a priority and which can be dropped if need be.
2. Plan a time cushion – for example, ample time for thoughts, questions and comments at different points and the end of each training session. This can be reduced if different discussions have taken longer. (Working to time schedules or taking the time the plan needs is, of course, going to be a cultural feature that will challenge different trainers in different ways.)
3. Design with potential adaptations in mind.

Something that wasn't discussed during the interviews (due to the absence of my explicit questions on the topic) was that an increasingly common context is that people are in different geographies and time locations, working flexibly or from home. There is more of a demand for asynchronous as well as virtual training. Some thoughts:

+ Are you able to deliver a programme that people can access at different times and have the same opportunity? Know your own skills and need for support.
+ Embrace technology. What platform(s) are you, or your client, using? Know how you and the participants will be supported.
+ Create different resources: reading, watching, listening, reflecting, writing, quizzing (variety appeals to different preferences whatever the type of training – in person, virtual, asynchronous).
+ Create networks. What mechanisms are you putting in place to facilitate discussion and sharing among the participants?
+ How are you are going to connect with participants? Do you need to?
+ As with all training, begin any design with the goal and outcome in mind.

Cultural intelligence is about people. What I have learned is that the conversations, reflections and aspirations about becoming more culturally intelligent are different in every training and coaching situation I find myself in. What I am sharing is a framework, then I'm leaning in to encourage and inspire people to use it.

Key takeaways

✧ Cultural intelligence requires all four capabilities. If you are sharing the CQ framework, ensure that you share all the capabilities. This doesn't mean you have to dedicate the same time to each; consider the context and purpose of the people you are with and adapt accordingly.

✧ Ensure you factor in planning time for your participants to think about how they will apply the training.

✧ Question any assumptions about which CQ capability is more important and design your training for the people, purpose and context you are going into, rather than your preferences.

✧ There are multiple approaches for developing other people's CQ. Experiment, take risks and seek feedback.

Questions to consider

✧ What has your experience been of developing your CQ?

✧ How are you assessing what the CQ of your participants might be?

✧ What is the culture in the context in which you are providing training?

✧ What other models, development tools and frameworks could it be useful for you to link CQ with?

✧ What are the key elements you want people to take away from training with you?

Chapter 11

AI and the future of cultural intelligence training

By guest author, Dr Lyla Kohistany

Note from Lucy: When I was training to become a master CQ facilitator, one of the master trainers I worked with was Lyla Kohistany, who was then employed by the Cultural Intelligence Center. When I came to think of people to interview for the book, Lyla was an obvious choice. I experienced how brilliant she is as a trainer, and she was completing a PhD titled, 'Listening to Leaders: Expanding cultural intelligence learning opportunities for US Army Special Forces'. As a veteran of the American military, she has experience of a different sector to everyone else I contacted. I was disappointed when, understandably, she had to withdraw from the interviews due to the demands of her PhD. The loss of that interview is your gain, as many had suggested to me that I should write about training and AI as part of this book. When Lyla asked how she could support this project, I knew she was the person I could ask to contribute this chapter as she has the experience I lack.

We discovered that we have a shared vision to create a network where cross-cultural facilitators come together to keep mastering their craft, share best practices and lessons learned, and create meaningful change in their respective workplaces around the world. More about that in the conclusion; first, here is Lyla's chapter about AI and CQ training.

Introduction

Imagine this, fellow facilitators: a world where your cultural intelligence educational programme has a built-in AI sidekick. It analyses communication styles near instantaneously, identifies potential misunderstandings before they erupt and even coaches on pronunciation in real time. Sounds like science fiction, right? Actually, no. It's today's reality.

I am a huge science fiction nerd who grew up with the *Alien* and *Terminator* global blockbuster franchises, which featured multiple artificially intelligent characters and two strong female leads. In fact, after my mother and brother, Ellen Ripley (the protagonist in the *Alien* movies, played by Sigourney Weaver) and Sarah Connor (the protagonist in the *Terminator* movies, played by Linda Hamilton) were the two biggest influences on who I became as a woman and a US Navy officer.

So, when I had the opportunity recently to visit Mas Des Infermières, Ridley Scott's vineyard and estate, which also houses movie memorabilia from the *Alien* movies he directed, I was overjoyed. With each step of the tour, I was increasingly immersed in the nostalgia of my childhood. As I walked past space suits used in the *Alien* franchise, I reflected on my simplistic judgements about AI as a child – Ash (the synthetic in *Alien* played by Ian Holm) was bad because he tried to hurt Ripley, while Bishop (the synthetic in *Aliens* played by Lance Henriksen) was good because he helped to save her.

But, as an adult watching Michael Fassbender in *Prometheus* and *Alien: Covenant*, I understood that AI, as with most of humanity's creations, can be a force for good or evil. The spectrum of AI reflected in these films – the ruthless Ash, the loyal Bishop, the enigmatic David and the obedient Walter, with the latter two androids being the same model but with vastly different programming – exemplifies the vast potential and inherent risks of AI. Just as these fictional AIs held varying purposes and personalities as programmed by the humans who designed them,

AI tools designed for cultural intelligence training can be powerful assets when implemented thoughtfully. So, let me assure you – AI isn't here to steal your job. It's here to augment your human expertise gained through years of experience and empower you to create even more impactful training programmes.

AI – our superpower sidekick

AI's true potential lies in its ability to supercharge training in a few key ways. It can help facilitators identify real-world challenges, develop scenarios to address those challenges, and tailor content and activities to individual needs and cultural backgrounds.

I use AI in a variety of ways in my projects. I begin by using AI-powered analyses of survey data to analyse vast amounts of text information from pulse and culture surveys as part of my initial needs assessment. Using AI enables me to quickly identify recurring themes, keywords and sentiment around cross-cultural challenges within an organisation. While survey instruments such as Qualtrics have built-in AI tools, you can also upload any exported survey data into software such as NVivo or Atlas.ti to streamline this initial but critical analytical step. Then, with this understanding of real-world themes facing the people within the organisation, you can better tailor your material and scenarios so they resonate with the participants.

Next, I use AI assistants such as ChatGPT and Gemini to brainstorm and refine role-playing scenarios for training simulations. Rather than relying on these AI assistants searching the internet alone and potentially providing me with incorrect information, instead I upload lengthy documents containing vetted cultural information about various countries and ask the AI to develop scenarios with dialogue for various personas. These AI tools can rapidly help create variations based on different cultural contexts, ensuring the scenarios are relevant to the organisation's specific needs. For designing presentations, I use AI-powered platforms such as Canva to quickly turn my documents into slides with compelling visuals, using the AI image generator. Based on the information I provide, Canva also creates poll and quiz questions to keep the audience engaged. You can even create short AI-powered videos!

For those facilitators working with larger participant groups or on longer-term projects that require you to teach/facilitate at scale with a geographically dispersed participant network, consider using virtual simulations so you can challenge participants to apply their knowledge and skills in diverse cultural contexts. Participants can virtually 'visit' a foreign country or have real-time conversations with AI-powered avatars representing different cultures, preparing them for the unpredictable twists and turns of real-world practice. You can develop your own virtual simulations using platforms such as VRdirect or work with an immersive learning experience provider such as Mursion to immerse participants in realistic scenarios and practise 'soft' skills. Even a demo of Mursion may help you begin thinking about how you can design your own cultural intelligence scenarios.

Additionally, AI can track participant progress throughout the learning pathway and suggest targeted interventions to ensure everyone thrives, allowing facilitators to provide individualised support at scale across large organisations. Learning management systems (LMS) such as EdApp and Docebo have built-in data analytics that trainers can leverage to track participant progress and identify areas for improvement in CQ training programmes.

While language (sociolinguistics) is just one aspect of cultural intelligence, many of my clients ask for resources related to language learning. Apps such as Duolingo or Babbel use AI to provide real-time feedback on pronunciation and grammar, which can be applied to role-playing exercises during training. For clients asking for support with learning English, consider recommending FLOW Speak, which uses AI to instantly provide feedback on pronunciation while teaching colloquialisms as well as formal workplace and educational setting vernacular.

The irreplaceable human touch

However, while AI excels at data and personalisation, it can't replicate the magic and mystery of the human brain. This is where your expertise as a master facilitator truly shines. You possess the ability to navigate the delicate nuances of humour, sarcasm and unspoken social cues that AI simply can't grasp. These subtleties are the lifeblood of effective communication, and your ability to navigate them is irreplaceable.

Building rapport with participants is another area where AI falls short. There's no substitute for the trust and connection a skilled facilitator fosters in the learning environment. After all, the goal of cultural intelligence and cultural intelligence education is for us to make and nurture ever deeper connections with other human beings. More personal connections will hopefully lead to fewer stereotypes because humans are like onions (and ogres from *Shrek*) – we have a lot of layers. I am Lyla. I am Afghan. I am American. I am a veteran. I am a Muslim. And based on my lived experiences, no AI can account for how someone should build rapport with me based on all these layers. Nor could that AI create the psychologically safe space we do as facilitators when we share aspects of our multi-layered identity and lived experiences that allow for open discussions, vulnerability and deeper cultural understanding. Ultimately, this is our role as human facilitators – a role no machine can play any time soon.

Finally, the ethical considerations of AI training can't be overstated. AI systems rely on datasets and coding provided by humans, who are inherently susceptible to biases stemming from their cultural, social and cognitive frameworks. Consequently, AI may reinforce existing stereotypes and inequalities, thereby undermining the very principles of cultural sensitivity and inclusivity that facilitators strive to uphold. As facilitators, we play a crucial role in ensuring that AI doesn't perpetuate cultural stereotypes or biases. It's up to us to guide the technology and ensure our programmes foster genuine understanding and culturally intelligent respect.

A powerful partnership for the future

The future of cultural intelligence training is about a powerful partnership that holds exciting possibilities. AI can handle large amounts of data and help you plan logistics, freeing you to focus on the human aspects: guiding discussions, fostering empathy and encouraging critical thinking. This dynamic duo of you and AI can create a more personalised, impactful learning experience for your participants, propelling them on their journey to becoming true CQ champions.

So, embrace the AI revolution. We are far from the day that humans are replaced by AI as educators, especially when it comes to a skill like cultural intelligence, which requires such constant attention and adaptability. However, human capital alone is not enough. The future of CQ training lies in collaboration between humans and machines. Today, we're already seeing augmented reality (AR), virtual reality (VR), mixed reality (MR) and natural language processing (NLP) revolutionise learning experiences. I imagine a future where cultural intelligence is a cornerstone of successful interactions, fostering empathy, understanding and innovation across borders and within communities. There simply aren't enough human facilitators to make this happen, but this is the future we can create by embracing AI as a powerful partner. Who knows, we may even achieve world peace... or at least avoid the (real-life) awkward moment when your Dari pronunciation results in calling someone a camel (*shutur hasti*) when you meant to ask how they are doing (*chutur hasti*). Duolingo can only take us so far – practising with a human makes perfect!

Key takeaways

✧ AI tools can enhance training by analysing large amounts of data, generating realistic role-playing scenarios and tailoring content to your specific audience/context.

✧ While AI can process and automate certain tasks, it cannot replicate the depth of human connection and nuance that you bring to training. Building rapport, fostering psychological safety and navigating complex social dynamics remain uniquely human strengths.

✧ AI systems are only as unbiased as the data and programming behind them. You must be proactive in ensuring AI tools do not reinforce stereotypes or cultural biases, instead guiding their use toward fostering genuine cross-cultural understanding and respect.

Questions to consider

✧ How can you leverage AI tools for needs assessments and data analysis as you begin developing and designing your CQ training programmes?

✧ How can you integrate AI-powered simulations and language learning apps into your training design?

✧ How will you ensure ethical considerations are addressed when incorporating AI tools in your CQ training?

Chapter 12

Questions from participants

n preparing for this book, I asked many people (in person or within LinkedIn groups) what they would like to be included in a book for people who provided training in cultural intelligence. Many said they would like to hear how others responded to some of the questions they received from participants.

This is a collection of the most frequently asked questions I received from those conversations.

- Can developing CQ really enable people to navigate the complexity of culture?
- Can you really improve someone's CQ Drive?
- How do you build the CQ of people who are not in the training room? And does your response change if they are leaders, people they lead or peers?
- How can you build or maintain CQ Drive when it seems our leaders just don't care?
- How do you know when it is a cultural or personality difference?
- What is the culturally intelligent way to deal with profound ethical differences?
- Who should adapt?
- How can you be authentic if you are always adapting to the cultural norms of others?
- Is CQ just for individuals or can an organisation become culturally intelligent?

You could receive the same question multiple times and respond differently, depending on many factors. These factors may include, but aren't limited to:

- whether you are in a group or one-to-one setting
- at what point in the training the question is asked
- how much time you have available
- what prompted the question (which can be a useful starting point for any response)
- what you are trying to achieve with your response (whether you are scene setting, establishing credibility, clarifying or expanding on something just shared, trying to shift or impact on group dynamics, for example).

Unless I specifically name an interviewee or use 'I', the answers are a blend of all the voices from the 11 interviewees. What I observed during the three months I was interviewing was that I changed, expanded or thought very differently about how I responded to some of these questions in ways my participants responded well to. I hope the same is true for you.

Can developing CQ really enable people to navigate the complexity of culture?

It is unsurprising that the interviewees were unambiguous in their response to this question. The answer was a direct and emphatic yes. Cultural intelligence is not an academic abstraction; it is a skill set. The interviewees all recognised this from their own experience and knew the academic research confirmed their experience was not unique.

It is useful to have a discussion on what is meant by culture or what the questioner is referring to if this question is asked. Many of us have a conversation about what the group of people we're working with understand by the word culture at, or near, the start of any training.

If you are receiving training in CQ, you are being given a framework onto which you can keep layering and building your strengths way beyond the end of any training programme. We are going to misread situations, even if we have been working in CQ our whole careers, but you can have confidence that continued application of the CQ capabilities will enable you to be better navigators of more and complex cultural contexts.

Can you really improve someone's CQ Drive?

As trainers, we do not have agency over the motivation of the people we are training. While the question 'Is it really possible to enhance your CQ?' drew an emphatic 'yes', questions about whether we can improve other people's CQ Drive drew a more thoughtful 'no'.

What we, and others, can do is excite and engage people with CQ. The interviewees talked about the need to be client orientated. What are the benefits or pain points for them? How do you ask questions, share data and use stories to reveal the intrinsic and extrinsic motivators?

However, another repeated point was that the motivation and reasons behind it had to be articulated by whoever you are seeking to motivate. Training is an invitation. Pay attention to how people are responding to your invitation and adapt where necessary, while also recognising what is your responsibility and what is the responsibility of others.

How do you build the CQ of people who are not in the training room? And does your response change if they are leaders, people they lead or peers?

What do you have agency over? This was a key consideration in the responses to these questions. Encourage people to focus on where they have agency. Only you can decide to develop your CQ capabilities – no one can do it for you.

Many of the interviewees had heard the frustration shared by participants that those who really needed to build their CQ or engage better across cultures were not taking the training. The main recommendation was to acknowledge the frustration and think through how you celebrate who is in the training and engage with potential benefits for them. If they were able to model and share the language, behaviours and benefits of being culturally intelligent, would that create opportunity to motivate others?

It can also be useful to play devil's advocate. When working in universities, for instance, I'm aware that groups often point to other groups who are not in the room as the source of problems, whether administrators pointing at the academics or academics pointing to the professional services teams and so on. It is always easy to see how others could improve and do better. Encourage whoever is in the training to commit to their development.

In Chapter 5, I shared thoughts on how to set the conditions during training for people to engage with and build their CQ. What agency do the people in your training who raise this question have in their organisational setting to create a place where psychological safety, wellbeing and vision are evident?

In summary, we can only invite others, create the environment, offer encouragement and possibilities, enable people to engage with their thoughts, words and reasons. We can model and share the benefits of CQ, but ultimately no one can do the work of self-development for others.

How can you build or maintain CQ Drive when it seems our leaders just don't care?

Questions suggested to get people thinking about this were:

* Does it serve you well to assume your leaders don't care?
* What possibilities would open up if you assumed that your leaders did care?

They may not know how to lead well, or what to do for the best, and there may be scope for you to give them a reason for engaging with cultural intelligence. What is the language of your leadership? What motivates them? What are they rewarded for? As Tom says, as humans we are often trying to move towards what brings pleasure and reward or away from pain and punishment. Will CQ help to make more money? Become an employee of choice? Free up time? Enable us to be more innovative? Can you highlight the rewards? Or is the lack of CQ resulting in unnecessary financial cost? A high staff turnover? Delayed project implementation or poor engagement (this could be with staff or external partners or agencies)?

Like everyone in an organisation, leaders are only human. Each role has its challenges and rewards. Culture impacts on how we view leadership and whether or not we would consider it our role to try to engage or motivate leaders. This brings us back to the key question: where do you have agency?

So much energy can be used in thinking about what others could be doing better, and it can be an avoidance tactic for not addressing it ourselves. However, people could also be in contexts where they don't feel that the leadership cares about them. People may need to hear that CQ is a choice and self-compassion is as important.

How do you know when it is a cultural or personality difference?

In the field of CQ, trainers will typically spend time developing a shared understanding of what the group understanding of culture is; fewer will discuss what is meant by personality. Depending on the group you are working with, personality, temperament and traits are all words that may be used, and you may want to do some exploring of what is meant when someone says 'personality'.

There were variations on this question which could come up during training sessions. One was, 'Why are we even bothering, as we are all just people. Culture is not what matters; just respond to the personality of the person in front of you.' Another was people thinking through, 'Do I need to respond differently if the behaviour is down to personality rather than culture?'

Some thoughts:

- **Sometimes (even most times, perhaps) you won't know.** Knowing a culture takes time. Do you have the time, a big enough sample and enough reference points to be able to work it out? If you only have experience of working with one person from any particular cultural group, perhaps the question is not useful.

* **Does it matter?** If you are noticing and responding to something that is different, does it matter where that difference stems from? The key question could be how you are going to go about working together and responding to your differences.
* **Why the binary – personality or culture?** Personality and culture are commingled. Our culture impacts on how certain personality traits may be encouraged or discouraged. While there are extroverts across the world, they may have been socialised to express that in very different ways in different parts of the world.
* **What is the situational context?** This is another useful dimension to add to this question. It may be less about culture or personality and more about events or experiences that have taken place. (Questions to consider could be: how do we respond to stress, or fear, or triumph? What other/external factors are having an impact?)

Two key themes in the responses shared by the interviewees were:

1. Culture is learned and it creates a shared pattern of behaviour, observable across a group or a percentage who are representative of a group.

Most of us forget that we ever learned to do many of the things we do every day. Basic things such as where our comfort with proximity to other people comes from. One factor is that we learn a cultural norm for how close to get to others when first meeting.

I used to play a game with American study abroad students in London, who were getting to know each other as well as having arrived in a new country. They each had to apply a sticker with their name on it to a blown-up balloon, keep the balloons in the air for a short period of time then find and have a conversation with the person whose name was on the balloon they caught at the end of the time. Then they'd have a conversation on a set question. After a couple of rounds, I would ask them to freeze and ask about things such as how they were spaced in relation to the person they were talking to. The groups were typically quite homogenous, from the same place in America, and it was rare for people not to be displaying the same space preferences when they faced a stranger to speak – ie two to three feet apart if face on; if closer, their bodies would be angled. Where there were variations we would discover that they knew each other really well or that they were from a different culture to the majority.

It created a useful point to start discussing why this was an observable pattern, where they learned it and whether they thought it would be the same everywhere. Exercises like this, where you can enable participants to view patterns that they perhaps take for granted, are especially useful with more homogenous groups.

Throughout a training session, it can be useful to observe patterns or behaviours and ask if that is part of the culture of the place (whether geographically or organisationally). Within a more diverse group, how can you know everyone's culture? Especially if you think that you have all been shaped by various cultural forces. If you have moved to a new location, it takes time to make the observations in order to know if behaviours are about personality or culture.

2. Don't make hasty assumptions about whether it is due to personality or culture, based on your own experiences and expectations.

You may project false interpretations when you assume personality or culture, which can impact on what you do next. For example, if you are from a culture where you have learned and it is expected that you would be explicit and say no if you were being asked to do something you could not do, when you work with colleagues who have learned that it is not polite to say 'no', especially to someone in authority, it can lead to negative judgements. Some of the interviewees had experience of people having been considered lacking in confidence or being evasive (typically by people from the West) because rather than say 'no', a more polite refusal for them was 'I'll try my best' (typically from people from Asian countries). If you have decided that someone lacks confidence, how will that impact on your future interactions?

The overall input from the interviewees was that this was a question most had heard, but as Samara said, 'We don't need to analyse the person. We just need to know where we are in terms of getting past our differences.'

What is the culturally intelligent way to deal with profound ethical differences?

This is a huge question – one several interviewees had experience of being asked, sometimes with the word 'ethical' replaced with 'moral'. Ethics are about which actions we consider are good for people and good for society. What it is to be moral, ethical, fair, honest and good is, of course, culturally relative. There is not currently much scholarship on the theme of cultural intelligence and ethics. (You may wish to keep your answer as short as this.)

There are various questions that may be useful to explore with the person who asked:

- Which ethical differences are the questioner thinking of?
- Is the question being asked because the person is engaged in a specific situation causing them an ethical dilemma?
- Is it a philosophical question, being asked in the abstract, in terms of what they have thought about a situation in another place which they have no involvement in?
- Is the questioner hoping to develop CQ as an approach to changing the ethics of others?

The conversation that flows from the questions above may determine if any of the following points are useful. There is always a need for time and patience when working across ethical divides. There is never a simple, quick answer as people, culture and ethics are all complex and it is worth stating this.

At one level, the responses from some of the interviewees were about using the CQ framework in a way that enables respect to be shown. It can be used as a tool to open up a conversation that enables you to explore and potentially rethink ethical stances.

What are the reasons why this person (or group) holds this view? Can you hold and work with these differences? What are the aims you hold that are above these differences? As Jennifer put it, 'How do we find that space above difference, where we begin to look at our own humanity and how we engage with each other?'

What are the shared goals? The focus here may be about customer satisfaction, patient care or organisational goals, and the examples given during these interviews were around clashes between different faiths, beliefs and political differences – the focus of discussion being on what enables us to carry out the goal without having to act in ways that are unethical to us, and showing respect for another when holding very different perspectives.

Cultural intelligence is not about changing the ethics of others, but creating bridges to relate to or work with others. Therefore people could change a behaviour in order to be more effective and inclusive and serve organisational goals without changing their beliefs. An example given was that using the pronouns a person requested was good customer service, or good for patient care, or an inclusive way to work with colleagues, rather than a statement on personal views about gender.

However, the interviewees also spoke about how there is a limit to everything, including CQ. What I noticed was that their responses were rooted in their context and experiences. Some referred to political or religious differences taking place in contexts where there is peace, whereas others were responding to experiences linked to war and conflict. What all of them spoke to was the need to know their own red lines, ranging from whether they were being asked to engage in an activity they considered unethical, to being put in the position of feeling they had to support specific wars, to being in places where their way of being was considered immoral or even illegal (sexuality was mentioned several times), or just profoundly different in the ways people are treated.

CQ is a choice. There are other choices, such as self-preservation, self-compassion and fighting for what you believe in, for instance. As someone who travels a lot said, it is OK to decide that there are some things you are not going to adapt to. If you are in a place in the world where you are able to ask yourself what is the culturally intelligent way to deal with this, that perhaps suggests some good fortune. Removing yourself from a situation may sometimes be the best option. Agency, safety and health are therefore aspects to consider, whether of the person asking the questions or any people they are asking to act in a specific way. Another element to consider is trust. Where there is fear, trust is a hard feeling to generate. What is the context of the person asking the question? Can ethical differences be discussed?

History is, of course, awash with stories of how there are shifts in what is considered ethical. Change does happen, both at an individual and a societal level, but it does not happen quickly or easily (or indeed in one direction). What are your non-negotiables? Knowing that, what options does it leave you with in this context?

What I am aware of is that among CQ practitioners, or sometimes when I'm training, people say it would be a better world if we were all culturally intelligent. Perhaps. Perhaps not. CQ is not ethics. It is not values. It is not how power is shared. CQ asks the question, did I achieve what I set out to achieve within this cultural context? There are multiple ethical positions. It is always going to be complex. As one interviewee said, this is the most challenging question in the collection and no one felt they had 'the' answer.

Think through your thoughts and which questions you would ask to help explore this. Some interviewees spoke to the importance of getting under the surface of potential requests for training to highlight if there are ethical concerns for you, or indeed if their issue is about ethical issues, in which case CQ on its own may not provide the results they perhaps anticipate.

Ensure that you have your own set of ethics. If you hold that profound ethical differences reveal a limitation, what can you then link CQ with to contribute to the changes you want to see in the world?

Who should adapt?

It depends! Perhaps unsurprisingly, this was the most repeated response. 'When in Rome, do as the Romans do' is a proverb I often hear, but the interviewees felt there wasn't a rule that was always perfect. While adapting to the culture you find yourself in may be a good guiding principle, there may be other considerations. There are, of course, also many different scenarios in which we are adapting to different cultures without visiting a different location.

What impact are you trying to have? Were you invited into a context in order to offer something different? (In which case, rather than adapting, explaining the difference may be more useful for everyone.)

Other questions to consider are:

- Who holds most power?
- Does adapting enable you to grow and develop?
- Would adapting be considered offensive?
- Is this about a short-term adaptation or is it a long-term adaptation? (What does the answer to this question raise for you?)

Only the individual has the capacity to decide whether or not they are going to adapt their own behaviour. I've heard Dr Linn Van Dyne, one of the co-founders of the Cultural Intelligence Center, say that the person with the most CQ will be the one who notices cultural differences at play and adapts.

However, the situation plays a large role. For example, a couple of interviewees who were consultants were clear that they had to adapt when they were pitching for contracts and delivering training in different organisations, for different roles, in different parts of the world. I'm only ever in someone's office because I've been invited in to discuss possibilities for delivering work. In the UK, the pattern is usually to offer a refreshment and have a couple of minutes of small talk (about the weather, travel or how we may know a shared connection, for instance). This is my preference. I'm also ready for people to get straight to business with no preamble, which used to throw me and I had to learn to expect and be prepared for different ways of starting meetings.

Stories were shared about the tension between business norms where quick financial gains were expected and those whose norms were about building a trusting relationship before any contracts could be agreed. The difficulty could lie in having to develop the capacity of the people in their teams and organisations to adjust their expectations rather than adapt to potential new partners or clients whose different way of doing business was understood. It's not just behaviours of individuals that may need to change, but team expectations, planning timelines, financial commitments, etc.

These examples lead to questions about impact and goals:

- What will be the rewards of adjusting?
- What will the cost of not adapting be?

It is often not about adapting across two cultural behavioural norms but about many, such as in international and multicultural teams. It is less about adapting to the norms of others and more about adapting to create the culture in a team that enables trust to be fostered and everyone to communicate and contribute well. Explicit conversations need to be had about communication norms and decision making, to reach agreements about how everyone is going to adapt to create a positive culture.

When an individual is asking for themselves, it can be useful to remind them that there is often a need to practise. Andrej has shared that he had to practise being a direct communicator to get his message across when leading international teams. It took time. It was uncomfortable at the start. Developing his ability to communicate directly did not stop him having a preference for indirect communication; it meant he was able to communicate and have the desired impact in more situations. It came from his desire to develop himself and adopt a growth mindset, which is important for developing new behaviours.

Adapting should come from a place of choice and confidence that the results are worth it. If you are adapting because you feel fear or unsafe, then perhaps there are considerations other than whether you should adapt or not. If you think others should be adapting, are you being kind in that judgement? Do they know that you hold that things could be done differently by them (and are you clear about how this would benefit everyone)? What are your options for influence? Could you interpret the situation differently?

How can you be authentic if you are always adapting to the cultural norms of others?

The interviewees had different experiences, depending on where in the world they worked, as to whether authenticity was raised by participants or not. The value placed on the concept of authenticity is cultural. Therefore this question may serve as a point from which to explore how the person's culture has shaped what is important to them. What are the cultural factors at play that make authenticity important to you? Catherine, who is French and lives and works in Singapore after many years in China, was blunt. In her experience, this is an individualistic question, asked when she has students from the West, rather than from students from Asia, which is typically collectivist.

In each context, from a young age people will have had different expectations. Were you encouraged to share your 'truth' and 'honest' opinion, or were you expected to adapt and match the context and the expectations of others? And to what degree? In which contexts?

Questions that were raised during responses to this question included:

♦ Who is the authentic you?
♦ Who decides if you are being authentic?
♦ In how many different ways can you be authentic?

What the interviewees stressed was that, rather than behaviours, core values were at the root of authenticity. Which raises the question:

+ Do you hold the assumption that your behaviours are your authentic self?

Catherine shared her experience of giving feedback in France, where criticism was generally understood as a way of giving information that would help someone else improve. Taking that approach in China led to people thinking she did not like them, was never happy with anything and always critical. It didn't help people improve, which was Catherine's hope; it made people retreat from her as their norm was that feedback should be delivered more softly, such as 'This paragraph could change a little' rather than pointing out what was wrong with the paragraph.

Do you have a sense that 'truth' is being honest and linked to being a good person? If this sense of being truthful is linked to being direct, you may then give both negative and positive feedback and consider them both equally useful for the person receiving it. It is worth remembering that when people are less direct, they are often listening for what is not being said; therefore they can pick up on feedback that is less direct in a way that someone used to direct communication will not.

Catherine wanted to support people in both contexts, but using the same behaviour with people familiar with different norms led to different outcomes and judgements. If she declared her authentic self to be a constructive and supportive person, people experiencing the same behaviours from different cultures would judge her differently.

Do you consider yourself to be effective? Kind? Inspiring? Caring? Inclusive? Knowing what you value and how you want others to perceive you is part of being culturally intelligent. Stay true to your ideas, thoughts and beliefs, but share them in a way the other person is capable of hearing, or set them up to be amenable to receive and process what you're saying. As Buhle and others shared, you can choose not to speak and still be authentic.

Many also shared that they had heard people say 'This is just who I am' and it seemed to be about justifying behaviours that were having a negative impact on others. This loops back to the question, who should adapt? If you are having a negative effect on others, what are the costs of that? Is that your intention? There are so many considerations in each interplay around issues such as power, safety and intent.

Jennifer shared that when she was asked this question, she would always want to affirm that the purpose of CQ is not about changing people. Whoever you are, you are good. The purpose is about being able to adapt and achieve goals. In the work she does, this is about developing inclusive leadership and fostering inclusive cultures.

In brief, core values are key. If you want to be kind, effective or whatever is important to you, which behaviour does that require? It is the behaviour, not your values, that changes. Adapting behaviour doesn't change who you are deep inside; it only changes how you respond to situations with the goal of bridging cultures.

Is CQ just for individuals or can an organisation become culturally intelligent?

This was a question that drew nuance from the interviewees. Half of them answered 'yes'. They were motivated by the belief that organisations can become culturally intelligent, enabling them to be inclusive and effective across multiple cultural contexts. Their view was that we can facilitate development that enables company culture to keep evolving and become culturally intelligent. For quite a few of the interviewees, their focus was not solely on individual change; the goal was organisational change. Their experience was that they had witnessed this change, which I'll caveat by saying that they saw it in the parts of the organisations they were working with.

CQ is about people. What is an organisation? People engaged in a common goal. Therefore develop leaders, develop teams, create processes, hold people accountable, keep the vision alive and relatable – and keep reflecting, building knowledge, planning and adapting using the CQ framework.

On the other hand, while no one said it wasn't possible for an organisation to be culturally intelligent, half were far more nuanced in their responses. What size of organisation are you thinking of? For some, size mattered, along with complexity, the scale of operations and different contexts. These were factors that some had found made cultural intelligence extremely difficult to achieve throughout an organisation, even when there were sizable pockets of it within the culture.

Lots of factors can impact on company culture and how things are done – staff turnover, expansion, cash flow, societal or political shifts, to name a few. As one interviewee said, you can create the intention, good processes and development, but typically you cannot mandate for someone behaving with cultural intelligence all the time (or perhaps even any of the time).

Another query raised was how to assess whether a company is culturally intelligent. The CQ assessments are great for individuals and teams, but there were question marks as to whether or not it was the right assessment to consider CQ at an organisational level, with the interviewees thinking that other tools were needed. There wasn't a suggestion about what to use instead, so perhaps there's a niche for someone to explore. Some thought that the CQ assessment does not link to contextual factors or goals and values, which are about more than managing to be effective across cultures and achieving what you set out to do.

Is your expectation that cultural intelligence improves social justice and inclusion? If so, it could be the case, hypothetically, that when you talk about the assessment tool, you can do an organisational report. You may see that the overall CQ Drive of the organisation is high. You may assume there is motivation and confidence to work across cultures, then discover there is not much understanding or engagement with the diversity that is represented in the society in which they are located. Would that suggest a culturally intelligent company to you? What metrics would you expect to see in an organisation declaring itself culturally intelligent?

This takes me back to the beginning of the book, when we were thinking about your motivation and the changes an organisation might want to see. In the third edition of *Leading with Cultural Intelligence*, there is a chapter devoted to building a culturally intelligent organisation, with David Livermore writing that it 'begins with linking CQ to […] mission, vision, values, and strategy, something that ties to the organisation's CQ Drive.'

My thoughts are that if we can travel in space, then it must be possible to create culturally intelligent organisations (and cultural intelligence is not needed to travel in space!). However, I don't think that is the point in and of itself. For me, it has to be rooted in values and intentions that create and enable organisations to contribute good to the world. And as I write that, I'm aware that you and I may have very different views on what 'contributing good to the world' may entail.

Key takeaways

✧ There is no one way to answer questions you receive. Keep an open mind to explore possibilities and link with the person and context you are in.

✧ Use questions in your response to explore what the person means by the words they use or the situation they are in.

✧ It is useful to develop your own community of practice so that you can think out loud and share perspectives on questions you receive.

Questions to consider

✧ Were there any responses to questions which surprised you in this chapter? What does that suggest would be useful for you to explore?

✧ Which participant question have you found challenging? What was challenging for you? How could you expand your thinking about the topic?

Conclusion

CQ is actually a pedagogy to challenge ourselves to be better people in this world. It's easy to teach, but it's very difficult for us to change. – Fenny Ang

The research is clear. Developing cultural intelligence enables us to relate and work more effectively where there is cultural difference. Writing this book emphasised to me that there are brilliant, committed people around the world engaged in similar work, whom you and I can share and learn with. I have interviewed 11 people and invited others to contribute, yet with each word written I'm aware that it is the word of one person who has only lived and worked within my own life. I can't be anything else. Each of the interviewees would have written different books from the same interview transcripts, and each suggestion could be weighted with so many caveats about place, people and purpose. With the same CQ framework, each of us will find a different way to share it. This is what makes each of you so important. The world needs people from different places, with different experiences, sharing cultural intelligence.

The process of listening to others, reflecting on my own practice and drawing from the experience of the interviewees has been enriching. The act of reflection also demonstrates that I have changed aspects of my practice. I hope I keep doing so, so that in my work sharing CQ, I keep growing and adapting so that I can be more effective. It is without a doubt easier to change when we have the support of others.

The questions I offered to you in the introduction were:

- What am I **learning**? (CQ Knowledge)
- What am I **thinking** differently about? (CQ Strategy)
- What **actions** can I take from this book? (CQ Action)

- How will this have **impact** for me as a trainer and the people I work with? (CQ Drive)

What are your responses to these questions?

Doing the work to create this book has emphasised to me the need to invest in my networks as key to me developing both my CQ and my training capability. I'm thinking differently, not just about the training, but also about advocacy for the work we do. As Catherine said, each of us is but a drop in the ocean, but we can each share stories with our networks, on social media, in our organisations, so that the drops can start bonding to create something bigger.

Throughout my career, conversations and the sharing of ideas have sparked possibilities. Lyla and I share a vision to create a global network for those who provide training to enable people to work and relate well across cultures. Many of us work in isolation, yet it is when we connect that we have the best opportunity to develop and grow. Therefore we are creating an innovative, collaborative community of practice, so that you can connect with others who face similar challenges and opportunities, sharpen your skills, share experience and expertise, trial approaches and collaborate.

We invite you to find out more about Cross Cultural Catalysts via the information at the end of this book.

Throughout my life, there have been substantial societal shifts, political changes that upended expectations, acts of horror and reasons to be optimistic. That process of change has not stopped while I've been writing, and some of the interviewees are operating in an environment more hostile to their purpose than the one they were in when interviewed. What has remained consistent is that our societies need people who are more culturally intelligent.

Keep learning.

Keep growing.

Build your community of practice.

However you go about developing and sharing cultural intelligence, I wish you well.

Cross Cultural Catalysts

Lyla and I invite you to find out more about our vision to create a global community where we can come together to master our craft, share best practices and lessons learned, and amplify our impact.

This comprehensive platform of community, content and collaboration will create a home for those of us who work with cultural intelligence as an approach to developing ourselves and others.

Find out more by scanning this QR code:

Or go to crossculturalcatalysts.com

Appendix

All the interviewees have a LinkedIn profile. You can also discover more about them at these websites:

- Tom Verghese: culturalsynergies.com
- Fenny Ang: coaching4real.com
- David Livermore: davidlivermore.com
- Andrej Juriga: culturalbridge.sk
- Sandra Upton: uptonconsultinggroup.com
- Justin Ngoga: impactroute.org
- Anindita Banerjee: in.linkedin.com/in/banerjeeanindita
- Catherine Wu: linkedin.com/in/drcatherinewu
- Samara Hakim: culturgrit.com
- Buhle Dlamini: buhledlamini.com
- Jennifer Izekor: abovedifference.com
- Lyla Kohistany: linkedin.com/in/lylakohistany
- Lucy Butters: lucybutters.com

Acknowledgements

There are so many people who contributed to this book and so many places I could start with my thanks, so I am going to start at home with my wonderful husband. I lucked out when you came into my life and chose to give me love, rock-steady support and encouragement. When I was full of doubt about my ability to ever complete this book, you would say, 'You're the woman who started a business with pre-school triplets in the house, and that business is still thriving. Of course you'll write a book.' You're always willing me on and letting me know you love me regardless. Thank you, Ian.

As for our sons, David, Thomas and Matthew, I can't claim you helped me to write in a practical sense (although when you all left for university in September 2024, there was more quiet writing time available). What you have given me, though, is a profound sense of purpose and belief that the future will be better for having you in it.

I wouldn't be doing the work I do now if I hadn't had the privilege of attending CQ training and events led by Dr David Livermore. In a host of different settings, David has consistently modelled and shared CQ in ways that continue to inspire me. It was as a CQ Fellow, a programme David created and leads, that this book took shape. I owe him many thanks for the generous guidance, suggestions and encouragement he gave me throughout the writing of this book – not to mention his quick acceptance of my invitation to be one of the interviewees.

Thank you to all the interviewees who shared and gave their time and trust to me. Tom Verghese, Fenny Ang, Catherine Wu, Anindita Banerjee, Andrej Juriga, Jennifer Izekor, Justin Ngoga, Buhle Dlamini, Samara Hakim and Sandra Upton – without you there would be no shared insights. Lyla Kohistany, I completely understood why, when writing your PhD, you didn't have the headspace to be interviewed. That you came back to me when you had completed your PhD to ask how you could contribute speaks volumes about the person you are. I am so excited to be working with you to create a network that supports, develops and encourages trainers in this field.

All of us have a debt of gratitude for the research into cultural intelligence, especially to Professor Soon Ang and Dr Linn Van Dyne. Your work has enriched so many lives – thank you.

Cherron Inko-Tariah MBE, your voice asking 'Why are you not writing a book, Lucy?' has stayed with me and I've appreciated the times we have spoken and you shared your experience of becoming an author. You planted the seed.

A big thank you to my CQ Fellow mastermind peers, who helped me shape the scope and purpose of this book – Mike Newton, Allison Coventry, Kristal Walker, Rahn Franklin and Margaret Page. Beyond the CQ Fellows, I have the sense of being in a CQ family. So many of you inspire and encourage me.

Thanks to those who read early drafts and gave me both encouragement and useful feedback –especially Dr David Livermore, Dr Linn Van Dyne, Dr Michael Goh, Trisha Carter, Marc Geil and Mike Newton. There were also many who kept checking in to ask how the writing was going and cheering me on. Thanks to you all, especially Vicky Lewis, Madelaine Webster and my brother Derek for his constant enthusiasm! And being given the keys to your flat on the Isle of Bute when I needed to get away and focus was a huge help, Jo and David Cook.

I want to say thank you to British Council colleagues, especially those from the British Council InterAction Leadership in Community Development team (2007–2010). Questions were such a major feature of this programme and it continues to inspire and shape the way I do things. Special thanks go to Caroline Khalaf (Palestine), Nour Al Rasheed (Jordan), Liz Zeidler (England) and Alison Jeffrey (Scotland). Thanks too, to Kate Sullivan (Singapore) and Ruth Nadja (Scotland) for the engagement and discussions while developing then delivering the Intercultural Fluency programme.

A special thanks to Mark Simmons, who was my manager when I joined the British Council in 1998. We have now had decades of fun and friendship, with you always encouraging me. I enjoyed all the times your London home served as a writing base for me.

I loved how, when joining The Right Book Company, I suddenly had a helpful, guiding, motivating team around me. Thank you Sue Richardson, Beverley Glick, Paul East, Andrew Chapman, Natalia Fantetti and Nick Redeyoff. And thanks to Mel Sherwood for the recommendation.

At the start, when I first had the idea for the book, I received so much encouragement from Viviane Vicente, a CQ master facilitator. I learned so much from working alongside her and conversations with her. She wanted to read it all, but cancer claimed her faster than I could write. Viviane, you are so missed. I remember when your emails switched from being addressed to 'Dear Lucy' to 'Dearest Lucy'. It went against all my Scottishness to reciprocate; so now, too late, I say thank you, dearest Viviane.

Notes

Introduction

Ang, S & Van Dyne, L (2009) 'Conceptualisation of cultural intelligence', *Handbook of Cultural Intelligence: Theory, measurement and applications* (eds, Ang, S & Van Dyne, L). Routledge.

Pink, D (2010) 'Rules for writing'. URL: danpink.com/2010/03/7-rules-for-writing

Chapter 1

Hofstede, G (1991) *Cultures and Organizations: Software of the mind – intercultural cooperation and its importance for survival.* McGraw-Hill. The 2010 edition was co-authored with Hofstede, G J & Minkov, M. See also: news.hofstede-insights. com/news/what-do-we-mean-by-culture

Sternberg, R J, Forsythe, G B, et al (2000) *Practical Intelligence in Everyday Life.* Cambridge University Press.

Ang, S (2021) 'Cultural intelligence: Two bowls singing' in Chen, X & Steensma, H K (2021) *A Journey Towards Influential Scholarship: Insights from leading management scholars.* Oxford University Press, p46. See also the short film *Two Bowls Singing*, URL: youtube.com/watch?v=hm5Fa9x3GaM

Dobbin, F & Kalev, A (2022) *Getting to Diversity: What works and what doesn't.* Harvard University Press, pp16-34.

Earley, P C & Ang, S (2003) *Cultural Intelligence: Individual Interactions Across Cultures.* Stanford University Press.

Sinek S (2011) *Start with Why: How great leaders inspire everyone to take action.* Penguin. Key concepts are in his TED talk: ted.com/talks/simon_sinek_how_great_leaders_inspire_action

Chapter 2

Livermore, D (2024) 'Cultural intelligence research you can use now'. URL: davidlivermore.com/2024/02/07/cultural-intelligence-research-you-can-use-now

Chapter 3

Maxwell, J C (2013) *Everyone Communicates, Few Connect.* Thomas Nelson Publishers.

Chapter 4

Maleki, A & de Jong, M (2014) 'A proposal for clustering the dimensions of national culture'. *Cross-Cultural Research* vol 48(2) pp107–143.

Livermore, D (2013) *Expand Your Cultural Borders: Discover 10 cultural clusters.* CQ Insights Series, Cultural Intelligence Center.

Dlamini, B (2024) URL: linkedin.com/feed/update/urn:li:activity:7181975752429469696

Chapter 5

Ang, S, Van Dyne, L & Koh, C (2006) 'Personality correlates of the four-factor model of cultural intelligence'. *Group & Organization Management* 31(1) pp. 100–123.

John Kotter is an American author of 18 books, Harvard professor and founder and chairman of Kotter International Inc. *Our Iceberg is Melting* (2006), *Leading Change* (1996) and *Accelerate* (2019) are recommendations from some of the interviewees.

Livermore, D (2016) *Driven by Difference*. Amacom.

Chapter 6

Livermore, D (2024) 'Cultural Intelligence: Three proven ways to measure it'. URL: davidlivermore.com/2024/07/10/cultural-intelligence-three-proven-ways-to-measure-it

Hall E (1981) *Beyond Culture*. Anchor Books, p39.

Watson, K S, Barker, L L & Weaver, J B (1995) 'The Listening Styles Profile: Development and validation of an instrument to assess four listening styles'. *International Journal of Listening* 9, pp1–13.

Livermore, D (2016) – see Chapter 5.

Livermore, D (2013) – see Chapter 4.

Hofstede, G (1991) – see Chapter 1.

Ang, S (2021*)* – see Chapter 1.

Chapter 7

Rockstuhl, T & Van Dyne, L (2018) 'A bi-factor theory of the four factor model of cultural intelligence: Meta analysis and theoretical extensions'. *Organizational Behavior and Human Decision Processes* 148. URL: drive.google.com/file/d/1cyqNicmui1W9E3xaVTABtn-Re-z6-umm/view

Kahneman, D (2013) *Thinking, Fast and Slow*. Farrar, Straus and Giroux.

BBC (2021) 'How to reset your brain with your breathing'. URL: bbc.co.uk/programmes/articles/1mW6885X3N2gKnVjXT00KCj/how-to-reset-your-brain-with-your-breathing

Eurich, T (2017) *Insight: The power of self-awareness in a self-deluded world*. Macmillan. View a short summary here: linkedin.com/pulse/only-15-people-truly-self-aware-heres-how-change-the-forem-co-hn98e

David-Barrett, T (2024) *Gendered Species: A natural history of patriarchy*. Independently published.

Rothman, J (2014) 'The origins of "privilege"'. *The New Yorker*. URL: newyorker.com/books/page-turner/the-origins-of-privilege

McIntosh, P (1988) 'White privilege and male privilege: A personal account of coming to see correspondences through work in women's studies'. URL: wcwonline.org/images/pdf/White_Privilege_and_Male_Privilege_Personal_Account-Peggy_McIntosh.pdf. This comes with notes for facilitators.

Deardorff, D K (2020) *Manual for Developing Intercultural Competency: Story Circles*. UNESCO Publishing. See also: unesco.org/en/enabling-interculturaldialogue

Bendix, A (2024) 'Writing by hand may increase brain connectivity more than typing, readings of student brains suggest'. NBC News. URL: nbcnews.com/health/health-news/writing-by-hand-may-increase-brain-connectivity-rcna135880

Chapter 8

Gaynor, Z & Alevizos, K (2019) *Is that Clear? Effective communication in a multilingual world*. Acrobat Global.

Gaynor, Z, Alevizos, K & Butler, J (2020) *Is that clear? Effective communication in a neurodiverse world*. Acrobat Global.

Duhigg, C (2012) *The Power of Habit: Why we do what we do and how to change*. Random House.

Agarwal, P (2022) *Hysterical: Exploding the myth of gendered emotions*. Canongate.

Chapter 9

Berger, W (2014) *A More Beautiful Question: The Power of Inquiry to Spark Breakthrough Ideas*. Bloomsbury.

British Council and Interaction Facilitation Team, 'Interaction: Leadership in community development Near East, North Africa & UK. Participant Manual 2009/10'.

Carter, A J, Croft, A et al (2018) 'Women's visibility in academic seminars: Women ask fewer questions than men'. *PLoS ONE* 13(9). URL: journals.plos.org/plosone/article?id=10.1371/journal.pone.0202743

Weingarten, E (2019) 'Who asks questions, and what it tells us'. *Behavioral Scientist* 19 June. URL: behavioralscientist.org/who-asks-questions-and-what-it-tells-us

Clean Change (nd) 'The basic Clean Language questions of David Grove'. URL: cleanchange.co.uk/clean-language-questions-of-david-grove

Covey, S R (2020) *The 7 Habits of Highly Successful People*. Simon & Schuster Ltd.

Kline, N (2002) *Time to Think: Listening to ignite the human mind*. Cassell.

Watson et al – see Chapter 6.

'What's Your CQ? Participant Guide (v.6.0)', Cultural Intelligence Center LLC ©2005–2024.

Chapter 10

Ramroop, M (2025) *Building Inclusion: A practical guide to equity, diversity and inclusion in architecture and the built environment*. Routledge.

Meyer, E (2016) *The Culture Map: Decoding how people think, lead, and get things done across cultures*. PublicAffairs.

Kotter, J & Rathgeber, H (2006) *Our Iceberg is Melting: Changing and succeeding under any conditions*. Macmillan. See also: kotterinc.com/methodology/8-steps

Chapter 12

Livermore, D (2024) *Leading with Cultural Intelligence The real secret to success*. Third edition. HarperCollins Leadership, p200.

About the author

Lucy Butters is a Master Facilitator in Cultural Intelligence and a CQ Fellow. She has been working to support organisations to be more inclusive and internationally effective since founding her training and coaching company Elembee Ltd in 2010.

As a CIPD qualified trainer, one of Lucy's passions is working with trainers and facilitators to develop and enhance their CQ training capability.

She has previously worked for the British Council in international cultural relations roles linked with developing and implementing strategy to support the international ambitions of universities in Scotland.

Lucy lives in Glasgow with her husband and as parents of triplet sons they are frequently reminded of the need to adjust thinking, actions and expectations.

EU Safety Representative: euComply OÜ Pärnu mnt 139b-14 11317 Tallinn
Estonia hello@eucompliancepartner.com +33 756 90241